EVENT HORIZON

☾

NEW & SELECTED

LATER POEMS

BY

ROBERT PACK

BOOKS OF POETRY BY ROBERT PACK

All One Breath
GREEN WRITERS PRESS

Clayfeld Holds On
UNIVERSITY OF CHICAGO PRESS

To Love That Well
LOST HORSE PRESS

Laughter Before Sleep
UNIVERSITY OF CHICAGO PRESS

Still Here, Still Now
UNIVERSITY OF CHICAGO PRESS

Composing Voices
LOST HORSE PRESS

Elk In Winter
UNIVERSITY OF CHCAGO PRESS

Rounding It Out
UNIVERSITY OF CHICAGO PRESS

Minding The Sun
UNIVERSITY OF CHICAGO PRESS

Fathering The Map
UNIVERSITY OF CHICAGO PRESS

Before It Vanishes
GODINE, PUBLISHER

Clayfeld Rejoices, Clayfeld Laments
GODINE, PUBLISHER

Inheritance
GODINE, PUBLISHER

Faces In A Single Tree
GODINE, PUBLISHER

Waking To My Name
JOHNS HOPKINS PRESS

Keeping Watch
RUTGERS UNIVERSITY PRESS

Nothing But Light
RUTGERS UNIVERSITY PRESS

Home From The Cemetery
RUTGERS UNIVERSITY PRESS

Guarded By Women
RANDOM HOUSE

A Stranger's Privilege
MACMILLAN

The Irony of Joy
SCRIBNERS

BOOKS OF LITERARY CRITICSM

Willing To Choose: Volition and Storytelling in Shakespeare's Major Plays
LOST HORSE PRESS

Belief and Uncertainty In the Poetry of Robert Frost
NEW ENGLAND UNIVERSITY PRESS

The Long View: Essays in the Discipline and Hope of Poetic Form
UNIVERSITY OF MASSACHUSETTS PRESS

Affirming Limits: Essays on Morality, Choice, and Poetic Form
UNIVERSITY OF MASSACHUSETTS PRESS

Wallace Stevens: An Approach to His Poetry and Thought
RUTGERS UNIVERSITY PRESS

EVENT HORIZON

☾

NEW & SELECTED
LATER POEMS

by

ROBERT PACK

Introduction by
PAUL MARIANI

GREEN WRITERS PRESS *Brattleboro, Vermont*

Printed in the United States

10 9 8 7 6 5 4 3 2 1

Green Writers Press is a Vermont-based publisher whose mission is to spread
a message of hope and renewal through the words and images we publish.
Throughout we will adhere to our commitment to preserving and protecting
the natural resources of the earth. To that end, a percentage of our proceeds
will be donated to environmental and social justice activist groups. Green
Writers Press gratefully acknowledges support from individual donors, friends,
and readers to help support the environment and our publishing initiative.

Giving Voice to Writers & Artists Who Will Make the World a Better Place
Green Writers Press | Brattleboro, Vermont
www.greenwriterspress.com

ISBN: 978-1-950584-96-3

PRINTED ON RECYCLED PAPER BY BOOKMOBILE.
BASED IN MINNEAPOLIS, MINNESOTA, BOOKMOBILE BEGAN AS A DESIGN AND
TYPESETTING PRODUCTION HOUSE IN 1982 AND STARTED OFFERING PRINT SERVICES IN 1996.
BOOKMOBILE IS RUN ON 100% WIND- AND SOLAR-POWERED CLEAN ENERGY.

*This book is dedicated to the memory of my mother, Henrietta,
and to my wife of sixty years, Patty.*

With special thanks to my longtime fiend James Zanze.

EPITAPH

Here lies Bob Pack who never could retire,
he had too many ironies in the fire.

CONTENTS

From *Clayfeld Rejoices, Clayfeld Laments* (1987)

From *Before It Vanishes* (1989)

From *Inheritance* (1992)

FROM *Fathering The Map* (1993)

FROM *Minding The Sun* (1996)

FROM *Rounding It Out* (1999)

From *Elk In Winter* (2004)

From *Composing Voices* (2005)

From *Still Here, Still Now* (2008)

From *Laughter Before Sleep* (2011)

From *To Love That Well* (2013)

From *Clayfeld Holds On* (2015)

From *All One Breath* (2019)

Event Horizon (2021)

INTRODUCTION

WHAT AN EXTRAORDINARY GIFT Robert Pack, who has blessed us with poems for the past sixty-five years, has given us in this, his most recent volume! Where to begin?

Let's begin with the strange, even unsettling title of Pack's new volume: *Event Horizon*. It's an astronomical term, it turns out, and signifies "a theoretical boundary around a black hole beyond which no light or other radiation can escape." In other words, a point of no return. And there you have it, Pack at his canniest, most quizzical, most plangent, and at the same time comic.

And make no mistake: these poems will bear all those resonances and radiations out.

There's the eco-friendly Bob Pack, heir to the tradition of Wordsworth. You can feel the very air of Montana in these poems: in the snow geese returning home once again, in the dwindled herds of Montana bison, in the poignant image of his daughter, Pamela, existentially alone on one of those mountain cliffs she has been climbing over the years, hanging on only by her fingers and toes hundreds of feet above ground level as a hawk sails hovering below her and evening comes on.

Take the opening poem here, "Whiteness," where the snow keeps coming at you until you are dissolved." "It was snowing, and it was going to snow," Stevens wrote a century ago. But of course the snow keeps coming, accumulating

on pines, on firs,
on spruce, on tamaracks,
on broken stalks
and twisted shrubbery.

Keeps falling in Condon, Montana, as it does in Hartford
and New York City, easing down "on fields, on hills,/ on moun-
tain slopes,/ on ice-locked riverbanks," on barns and roofs and
fences, along which an old man trudges along, the misery of it
as it falls

on perching ravens' wings,
the backs of browsing horses
and on stationary elk.

Ah Montana! An old man who lost his father all those years ago,
like Hamlet making out his father's ghost returning only now

to finish what he had left unresolved —
forgiving his own brother's stealing from their partnership.

"Forgiveness time," John Berryman wrote in his last years,
as now Pack does, hoping to mend what in truth can never be
amended. You can hear the palatable sadness here, as you can in
Johnny Cash or the Psalms written in the desolation of Babylon,
or Shakespeare's Lear or those women wailing at the close of
the Iliad as their beloved Troy and their men and their children
go up in smoke.

Then, too, there are the consolations of those poems where
the poet imagines his son, Erik, like another son carrying his
father, old Anchises, as now Erik helps his aging father settle into
a canoe, the two rowing out into the glacial lake, or hiking high
in the pine- and birch-studded mountains. Consider other poems
as well, where the poet's grandson appears, the old man eager to
teach the boy how to pitch a curveball or field a grounder. Add
to these those heart-wrenching memories of the father he lost
and of an aging mother and of a beloved sister back there in the
Bronx all those years ago, and soon we, too, are caught up in the
web of life's unenviable and inevitable losses.

Add to these Pack's poignantly comic poems, as when an old

man admires the nearly-transcendent beauty of a young woman, or the old man making his way to his front door at Halloween to find a masked woman in an erotic hallucination whispering *trick or treat*, as the old man tries to figure what to do with that.

Then the poems to and about Patty, his wife for as long as he's been writing his poems. The truth is his humor and wit and kindness have been mainstays for me now for nearly half a century. Along with his George Burns/ Jack Benny humor and his outrageous puns, the way he packs his poems with puns over and over. As in *Sing, heavenly moose,* which, when he read it in Bread Loaf's Little Theatre years ago the poet Marvin Bell got up and booed him (with affection of course) until everyone, as it dawned on them what Pack—straight-faced of course—had just done, rose up and joined the chorus.

To counter this comedic strain, there's the philosophical Pack, constantly questioning the meaning of it all, questioning God (if in your world—as in Berryman's or Hardy's or Frost's poetry—there is a God for you to address) even as the years and months and days slip from us, urging us to make up our minds while there's still time. For me, at least, Pack's poems keep echoing a recurrent theme from the Book of Ecclesiastes, which is something he and I across the table have mused upon and discussed so many times over the years, most recently in Rabbi Ravi Shapiro's translation, "For that which befalleth the sons of men befalleth the beasts . . ."

And then are those allusions to Freud and Darwin, whom he has studied over the years, as well as his long interior dialogues with his old pals, Shakespeare and Milton and Keats.

And of course there's the language: the sheer sublimity of his evocations of nature, as Harold Bloom noted years ago, a language filled with the beauty and sadness inherent in our consonants and vowels. It's a language which for me evokes the worlds of Hart Crane's *White Buildings* and Wallace Stevens's *Auroras of Autumn.* Or think of Charlie Chaplin or Jimmy Durante, saying goodbye to his audience, then turning and fading away as he exits, while the circle of the screen narrows and then—inevitably—goes black.

There are so many wonderful stories he has given us over the years, which go hand in hand, as they must, with the very way in which he tells those stories, whether in trimeters or tetrameters or pentameters, Formalist that he is. His sonnets strike me as so subtle and so right, like his rhymed stanzas and his mastery of the blank verse line. And, as always, there's the straightforward way he enters into a poem, something which reminds me time and time again of one of his favorites, Robert Frost:

> Driving me home from yet
> another visit to the eye doctor,
> my wife took the old farmland route,
> and there across a field of corn,
> stretching from east to west,
> a rainbow's arc appeared . . .

And we're back to the world of Noah and Genesis and Leviticus once more, and that heard and unheard music suffused with the poet's profound understanding of suffering. Not only human suffering, but the suffering of animals, who have no language with which to express their suffering, beyond a howl or whimper or—more poignantly—silence.

And then there's his wife Patty again, helping him back into the house and standing him on his walker, old soldier that he is, with a storm outside threatening to drown everything. And then, voila!, the beautiful dreamlike ending of the book, where Patty opens the door to let the animals in, two by two: "the white-tailed deer,/ foxes and wolves, red squirrels, bobcats," and the frolicking rest.

Here then is our covenant with creation: to care for the vulnerable. All of which somehow manages to touch on the beauty and majesty of what Bob Pack's poems have wrought for us yet one more time. These poems, dear reader, are a powerful testament to the human imagination, poems where I can hear Stevens and Yeats and even canny Shakespeare applauding, there, somewhere in the rafters, in those rumbling sounds that seem to speak like thunder like some Event Horizon.

Paul Mariani, October 2019

FROM

Waking to My Name

(1980)

☾

AFTER RETURNING FROM CAMDEN HARBOR

With the idea of water still in mind,
I say these words out loud and know, therefore,
that I am riot asleep; furiously
my mind seizes on green things to assert
its wakefulness: a plain, translucent pitcher,
quiet with milk, on a yellow tablecloth
brightened by morning sun. I observe my lawn,
as if asleep, hazy and steaming with dew
like a white sea sparkling green, according
to the soothing words of my idea of water,
though thunderclouds gathered furiously
over Camden Harbor with sailing boats
rearing like horses against the flat slap
of foaming waves. What stirs my wakefulness
is my idea of you who challenge me
to break free from my tightening mind
that furiously defends itself with words—
on Saturday when water, green as my anger
slobbering like horses, whinnied and surged
from my mind's depths: the nightmare sea where words
are forever wakening, forever asleep.
And though I spoke them, they were not my words;
because my anger toward you at Camden Harbor
snorted and roiled like foaming water,
it seemed as if I stood there still asleep
repeating an idea someone else's green mind
furiously had brought forth. I did not
say what I wanted then to choose to say,
and so I could not feel what furiously
I wanted to feel, according to the idea
that love means choice or that we live asleep—
as beside the water shaking the dock
I failed to will to compose the words
that could free me from the sea-dream of my anger
into a chosen yellow breakfast scene
with a flowered cup and a green pitcher of milk

casting its shadow as you pour for me.
Leaving next dawn, awed from high Camden hill,
the stilled bay water seemed asleep, and we
drove on in sullen silence homeward
through shifting sea-green light of crowded pines
until, as if from nowhere, you explained
that a computer—given six random words
and the idea each sentence must include them,
all repeating in the final line—
composed a poem that furiously made sense.
Still angry, and yet wanting to please you,
a pitcher on a yellow tablecloth in mind,
I asked you what the six words were; you said:
idea water asleep furiously green words.

DEPARTING WORDS TO A SON

We choose to say good-bye against our will
Home will take on stillness when you're gone
Remember us—but don't dwell on the past
Here—wear this watch my father gave to me

Home will take on stillness when you're gone
We'll leave your room as is—at least for now
Here—wear this watch my father gave to me
His face dissolves within the whirling snow

We'll leave your room as is—at least for now
I'll dust the model boats that sail your wall
His face dissolves within the whirling snow
It's hard to picture someone else's life

I'll dust the model boats that sail your wall
Don't lose the watch—the inside is engraved
It's hard to picture someone else's life
Your window's full of icicles again

Don't lose the watch—the inside is engraved
A wedge of geese heads somewhere out of sight
Your window's full of icicles again
Look how the icicles reflect the moon

A wedge of geese heads somewhere out of sight
My father knew the distances we keep
Look how the icicles reflect the moon
The moonlight shimmers wavelike on your wall

My father knew the distances we keep
Your mother sometimes cries out in the night
Look how the icicles reflect the moon
The moonlight shimmers wavelike on your wall

My father knew the distances we keep
Your mother sometimes cries out in the night
The moonlight shimmers wavelike on your wall
One June I dove too deep and nearly drowned

Your mother sometimes cries out in the night
She dreams the windy snow has covered her
One June I dove too deep and nearly drowned
She says she's watched me shudder in my sleep

She dreams the windy snow has covered her
She's heard your lost scream stretch across the snow
She says she's watched me shudder in my sleep
We all conceive the loss of what we love

She's heard your lost scream stretch across the snow
My need for her clenched tighter at your birth
We all conceive the loss of what we love
Our love for you has given this house breath

My need for her clenched tighter at your birth
Stillness deepens pulsing in our veins
Our love for you has given this house breath
Some day you'll pass this watch on to your son

Stillness deepens pulsing in our veins
My father's words still speak out from the watch
Some day you'll pass this watch on to your son
Repeating what the goldsmith has etched there

My father's words still speak out from the watch
As moonlit icicles drip on your sill
Repeating what the goldsmith has etched there
We choose to say good-bye against our will

RONDO OF THE FAMILIAR

Beside the waterfall,
by the lichen face of rock,
you pause in pine shade to remember blue
for drawing back, and green
for trust, replenishing yourself
among familiar leaves
with scattered sunlight.
And beyond those trees in time not ours,
you see our children search
for what we gave them, only to find
our love again
in other hands and faces
where our bodies cannot go.
And I step forth
into the scattered light
where you elude me,
though my hands reach out
to share these daily losses,
each beloved breath rounded to a pause,
that still compose our lives.
And the waterfall spills on;
and lichen holds to the rock-face
in the slowness
of its quiet life, deliberate
as the dividing of a cell;
and you remember blue
for each round pause you made
freshening a bed,
washing a window with even strokes.
And I step forth
into quickening light
that restores you and
takes you away, telling my hands
to be true to their green truth—
as our children preparing
faithfully to depart

beyond those trees,
hold for an instant in the pause
you have composed for them.
And I enter that pause,
though the waterfall spills on,
and pollen dust stains
our windows, and the familiar bed
deepens its repeated sigh,
as you wait for me,
each loss fragrant in your arms,
blue as the early crocus
our children soon will stoop to,
pausing by a waterfall
in familiar time beyond us
in pine shade
by the lichen face of rock.

THE KISS

A glaze of ice glistens in the manure
and rutted mud of the plowed-under garden
as the brittle crack and squish of my greased boots
leads me plodding beside my vague reflection
this crisp April morning, as if my image
still were in the thawing earth I planted,
and last year's buried spring still stirred and shined
within the slick clay of the chunky soil.

With boot-grooves packed with mud, my cold cleft toes
imagine they can feel the rising moisture;
stopping by a three-year red delicious tree
to scrape a fresh bud with my fingernail,
I see that it is green inside-alive,
having survived the winter in my care.
Yes, it is soft and moist, it has come through
under my care, and I remove the wrapping-
aluminum foil and tape-around its trunk
that saved it from the gnawing mice and voles
who girdle fruit tree barks beneath the snow.
Now on the yellowed grass, the perfect turds
of starving deer, glimmering like planets,
circle the tree, and the faint waft of skunk
brushes me with a puff of wind; I like it,
it quickens my sense at the exquisite edge
where pleasure cloys, where one knows surely
what the human limits are. I kneel
beside another tree as if to dress
a child for school, snipping a dead branch
as sharp sun strikes the creased foil by my knee,
catches my dazzled eyes and makes them tear.
A stranger here might think I truly wept.

Spring blood sings in my veins even as it did
some thirty years ago when I planted
my first apple tree. No lessening

of pleasure dulls the sun's feel on my arms,
a warming chill, or the female curves I see
along the hill that fruit trees make when my eyes
follow slowly, caressing every slope,
then moving on. I am gathering my life in
now with a breath, I know what thoughts I must
hold back to let my careful body thrive
as bone by bone it was designed to do.

A gust of wind comes off the upper slope.
Having followed me, my youngest son,
crying, "Watch me, Dad!" runs along the ridge
much faster than I thought he could, launching
his huge black birthday kite; catching the wind,
the kite leaps for the sky, steadies itself
as the string goes taut. It glides above me, swoops,
floating its shadow on my squinting eyes,
which pruning snippers still in hand, I shield
from shocking light. Designed like a great bat—
hooked wings and pointed ears and long white fangs
grinning like Dracula—it swoops again,
eclipsing the sun, hovers, dives at me;
I see the mock blood oozing at its mouth
and random dribbles brightening its belly
just as it crashes in the apple tree.
I take more shining foil from the tree
and roll it into two enormous teeth,
set them in my mouth like fangs, and chase
my son across the field, running faster
than I thought I could until my ribs
smolder in my chest and my clay hooves ache .
He screams as if the demons of his sleep,
returning from the frozen underground,
were actually upon him—as I catch him,
grapple him down, sink my gleaming teeth
into his pulsing throat and suck, suck deeper
than I have ever sucked, tasting his life
sweeter than any apple I have known.

LOOKING AT A MOUNTAIN RANGE WHILE
LISTENING TO A MOZART PIANO CONCERTO

Looking eastward through my picture window
over the snow, the sun just down, I see
the mountain range hazing to one shade of blue;
now with the trees obscured, it is a sweep
of shape darkening so flat, one might not
recognize a mountain range at all—
its silhouette is just a wandering line,
drawn by a hand that might be falling asleep
or else so free that every arc it makes
of rise or fall expresses the contentment
that it feels at heart, although it leads
nowhere but on, and might as well drift off
into another range of farther blue.

Brightly the piano asserts its melody;
the orchestra gathers its colors to reply,
true to the law that everything responds,
nothing is left unanswered, that variation
extends the self—as if one's life were made
essential in a piano's theme, departing
then returning one to what one is.
And now again it is the piano's turn,
and now the separate instruments, again
as one, move onward to their chosen end
beyond which nothing else will be desired.

And so my ears pulse back into themselves;
my eyes return to seeing what they see:
the mountain's silhouette—a floating line
leading my sight where visible blue ends.
It is an end in thought—my life goes on,
here I am deciding what to play next
as you appear; suddenly, I recall
when I first saw you, twenty years ago,
playing your flute: I think of waterfalls

in moonlight, orioles in cherry trees.
Your smile extends the silence of your pause,
and then, as if unsure where to go next,
you walk adagio past me out the door,
just as I hear the piano enter in.

The mountain's silhouette is now less sharp.
Something seems missing as the record ends,
spinning with a hiss that empty space
must make between the stars. I move the needle
to the start and light the lamp above my chair.
There are no mountains anymore, only
my reflection in the picture window
like a surgeon's x-ray, ghostly and remote.

I hear the introduction once again;
the piano sings so freshly that I feel
the reason why the orchestra replies.
And you return, carrying the flute
your fingers have not graced for twenty years—
as if a poem had conjured up the past
to ease the fear of darkness and of chance.

The one star in the sky is not enough
to light the mountain range where darkness holds
the shape my window frame provides. Once more,
for the strings' sake, the piano states its theme;
the violins are moved, they love their part.

Although I cannot see the dark beyond
my mountain's dark, I won't leave love to chance;
I watch you in the window coming near
as if to the conclusion Mozart had in mind.

THE THRASHER IN THE WILLOW BY THE LAKE

Now I can tell you. Hearing the shrill leaves
Swishing with your hair, I can recall
Just how it happened: the air was thick and still,
Like now, and I could see the lake reflect
The thrasher in the willow tree. I paused,
Knowing that I could never make her change.

I told her that I thought no simple change
Could help—it was too late for help—but still
The thrasher in the willow tree had paused
As if it were an omen to reflect
What the lake desired so that I could recall
Myself in the stirred wind and fishlike leaves.

I stared at her among the willow leaves;
If she looked young or old or if some change
Showed rippling in her face, I can't recall.
I know the thrasher saw her when he paused
Over the lake as if he could reflect
Upon his past, stop it, and keep it still.

Like this I held her—she would not stay still.
I watched, just like the thrasher, as the leaves
Stirred in the willow tree, and then I paused,
Gasping for breath, to see the lake reflect
The blurring wind. Her face refused to change
Enough because she knew I would recall

That moment always, that I would recall
When her eye met the thrasher's eye—and paused,
And might have, but never did, let me change.
Her lake sounds gurgled with the fishlike leaves,
And if you listen, you can hear them still.
Listen, they call in the willow, they reflect

The crying of the lake, and they reflect
The words she might have said to make me change.
Maybe she said them, but I can't recall
Ever hearing them in the willow leaves
When the thrasher blinked and her eye went still.
You know now why I brought you here and paused,

And since I could not change when the sun paused
To reflect the thrasher's eye among the leaves,
The willow will recall your face when the lake goes still.

A MODEST BOAST AT MERIDIAN

No spring can follow past meridian.
—WALLACE STEVENS

If I embraced a horse, Baby,
with all my power,
its neck would stretch like a giraffe's
in one impassioned hour;
and if I nibbled your ear,
an elephant, trumpeting its charge,
would thunder through the forest
of your veins at large.
Take me, my girl,
at the least pleading, I am your own,
prepared to spread largesse among all beasts
who famish at the bone
and wish to freshen at my watering place
where bannered leaves parade the wind's reply:
Be fruitful and go multiply!
Honey, by God, I vow the rains
will swell your lettuce-patch;
the hens will chortle in their huts,
and every golden egg will hatch.
And if, poor mortal girl, the truth
is all that we can bear,
I swear that I'll concoct a yarn
for us to weave our winter bed in
now that lying youth is gone.

THE TWIN

He liked to fight. I can remember how
he hit me with a shovel on the beach
when we were four, and I still see the smirk,
when we meet now, that filled his face—as if
nothing has changed, although I know you think
he is a gentle and unselfish man.

He poked my eye with a stick—and that scared him;
we embraced and I forgave him then, and he
promised mother that he'd be more careful.
I tell you this because she knew he lied,
and that encouraged him. Don't let yourself
be fooled, he's more persuasive than I am.

Mother believed him since she had no choice,
he was her son, she had to love him, but she
told me, weeping, that brothers must be true
to their blood bond; she took my hand and I
was flushed and I agreed. She sat right there
on our old sofa just as you do now.

Your hair reflects the gold threads of your shawl—
that rich brocade brings out your elegance;
you have the cheekbones of a baroness.
Despite our failures, to a primal love—
like any mother's for a nursing child—
something in us aspires eternally.

Don't try to change. Your love for ideal love
shines from your forehead almost visibly.
If he could only see it, I would be
at peace and give my blessings as I should.
But he will hurt you just as he hurt me
unless you learn to hold some feelings back.

Give yourself time; don't marry him so soon.
Observe yourself observing him, and see
if underneath his surface ease you can
detect his opposite; it is my duty
as his brother to be the one who warns you—
people end up repeating what they are.

He liked to fight. I can remember how
we embraced, and I forgave him then, and he.
told me, weeping, that brothers must be true,
despite our failures, to a primal love;
but he will hurt you just as he hurt me.
People end up repeating what they are.

WAKING TO MY NAME

Behind me the woods fill with the clashing
      of fresh bird calls—
phoebe, chickadee, robin, wren—
      as the June sun
angles in as if to render visible
      the faint tart scent
of the red pine and the white pine, the cedar,
      the hemlock and the fir;
and behind me, as I wake hungry for my own
      flowing, slow arising,
the names keep pouring in—my grandmother
      Ida, my mother
Henrietta, my sister Marian, Patty
      my wife, Pamela
my daughter: their faces mingle and separate,
      age and grow young,
as their vowels on my lips, their consonants
      blunt on my teeth,
pluck them back into themselves, into
      the certain image
chosen by my heart again to remind me
      something of each one
has not been left behind, and will not change.
      And behind me the mist
releases edge by edge each rock, and twig by twig
      each shrub, and the mud
glistens as the mud glistened when my grandfather
      woke beside the stream,
and leaf by leaf the mist released the oak
      and its name, and the maple,
and Thomas, his only son, and my father's name, Carl—
      as the birch grove caught
the slant light where the starved fox stood transfixed
      beside a boulder
heaved into its place how many mists ago?

And my heart fIlls
with him, and Joseph, his name, quivers in the cold air
        silver with the aspens
as their glazed leaves lift in the hook of the wind
        as he wakes by Ida
and behind him the mist releases eye by eye
        the covey of quails
and the white-arced tail-bar of the grouse
        startled into flight.
And waking by Henrietta, Carl's mind flies off
        after his grandfather
whose name I have lost, and he follows him
        long into the mist
where, for the living sake of love—Patty,
        and Erik, Pamela, and Kevin, I
must not yet explore, where stones shudder
        in repose, and each tree
breathes its fulfilled life in the forever
        of its single time.
And the June sun dawns upon my hand—
        nails and knuckles,
fingers, veins and thumb—which reaches
        out to the scented woods
and the visible names that merge in the lifting mist
        of my wakening age,
as I fly forth to the radiant green field
        with phoebe and chickadee
clashing, and robin and wren, and my name pulsing,
        repeating with my blood
that most of the full of my life is behind me.

FROM
Faces in a Single Tree
(1984)

☾

EARLY AND LATE

I hear the phoebe; she's returned to her
same nest this year. Are you awake? I hear
the mountain ash tree shudder with its load
of honeybees—I feel it, and I smell
crab apple blossoms lifting on the wind;
they must be opening. Throughout the night,
perhaps the soft vibrating of the stars—
something kept startling me, as if I had
good news to tell you, but I can't think what
it is. We've lived together fifty years,
our lives are what they were. How long is it
since we've made love?—there, now at last it's said,
it's openly between us, though we've shared
the knowledge every time we've almost touched.
Like fifty years ago, before we first
made love, old age makes you forbidden now-
as if it were some potion we had drunk.
      I picture you on Grandpa's farm, sitting
beside a stream, watching the maple leaves,
yellow and red, riding the blazing foam.
My brother, with a sailboat on a string,
played on the other shore, and so I paused,
uncertain—should I try to kiss you now?
A sweat-drop blew across your cheek and left
a hieroglyph as if on sun-warmed stone.
I must have held the kiss too long, because
you drew back. "No, not now," your breathing whispered.
On the first night you nursed Paul at home,
I watched the lamp behind you make a line
of hazy light to shape your silhouette.
I'd never seen your features quite so still;
you looked like Grandma on her cameo.
I laid my head upon your arm; "Not now,"
you said, "1 don't think it will snow tonight."
I didn't ask if "Not now" was a sentence
meant for me, or for the coming snow.

Last night you called out in your sleep, and then
I dreamed you visited my mother's house;
you both were standing at the open door,
she in a purple, flowered dress, and you
in white with noon sun reddening your hair.
You argued, though I couldn't hear the words;
she blocked your way from getting in the house.
I watched, and from the attic window where
I knelt upon a box, thinking I was
a child, I saw my hands upon the sill,
swollen with old, blue veins. A man came out,
with no shirt on, palms covering his face,
his skin white where the fingertips pressed in,
his shadowed muscles flowing down his arms;
you took his hand and started off with him.
"Don't go," I shouted, "Please don't go!" He turned,
lowered his hands, and gazed back in the house.
The young man there—that's who I was, that's who
you left me for! He paused once more, and then
you walked together down a pathway toward
a windless lake, diminishing within
an arching row of willow trees. We're told
that's how we see the farthest galaxies,
receding almost at the speed of light,
and vanishing except for their "red shift."
So what we know is only where they've left from
empty millions of light-years ago:
a shift toward red in the prism's spectrum
of a telescope to prophesy the past.
        News of the past arriving in the night:
your hair in sunlight and your silhouette;
the phoebe's whistle, and the thick odor
of blossoms opening; wet wind settling
and merging with the soft hiss of the snow;
everything held still in the mind at once,
everything here, and lost, and being lost,
equally unfolding, equally gone.
The autumn berries of the ash tree glimmer

still orange in the January snow,
at nightfall, shifting into red; I see
them now. Before the cedar waxwings left,
they could not eat them all; some are still here,
shrunken and brown, still clinging to the tree.
And you are here, and what we were-is here;
news of the past, I smell it in the dawn.
I feel that if I tried to love you now,
I'd gather in your breath, and hold it in
my own, and speak red words, and find a way.

INHERITANCE

I'm worried that you want to go in debt
to me, buying yourself a partnership
in Arthur's firm. It's only two years since
you've earned your architect's degree. I know
he is your friend, but friendship's not engraved
in blood ... well, sons can't pay their fathers back
unless they give the same love to their sons,
and on until some final reckoning.
But what I care about is now—you're home;
it's been three winters since we've split some wood
together as we used to do, and there
are red pines I've transplanted from the field
I want to show to you. Just yesterday
a ruffed grouse crashed against the window;
mother decided it would make the right
Thanksgiving meal for your return. "It's like
the sacrificial ram, caught in the brush,
God gave to Abraham for Sarah's sake,"
was what she said. I let that pass; you know
what weight your mother likes to lay on things.
The last year you were home she got so damn
possessive that I found myself competing
for your love. And then I felt left out.
She has a stronger hold on you than I.
Some day you'll feel your own life flowing in
your son, and then your debt will be redeemed.
One cool October afternoon, when he
is splitting wood with you, and you
are resting on a stump beside the sumac
blazing in the last warmth of the sun,
he'll lake his T-shirt off, and as the axe
descends, you'll watch his shoulder muscles flex
and then release beneath his flawless skin.
A waterfall, you'll flow out of yourself,

and what you are will find its form returned—
as if the wind blew leaves back to the trees.

       Don't be embarrassed that I tell you this;
it hurts for me to fumble with the words,
but it hurts happily, and that's the best
I have to give. Since you've been gone, I've planted
blight-resistant raspberries, too much
for us to use, but mother says she'll send
you her preserves. It has been hard, without
your help, to get the apples sprayed. We hope
you'll find a place where you can work nearby.
Arthur would not approve of that. I doubt
he understands what homes are for; he left
his father's firm to start his own. That's why
your mother takes the grouse to be a sign
to cherish your return, and why she made me
spray the raspberries all summer long.

       We've got another hour before it's dark;
let's split more wood. The Farmer's Almanac
predicts subzero cold again this year.
The planet's changed. My father warned me: "Son,
the reckoning will come. Earth is our home
or else our grave." Those were his words. It was
a day like this, and we were raking leaves
still dazzling in their reds and golds. I stood
before him, naked to the waist, sweating,
imagining your mother, trying to decide
what I would say when I proposed to her.

GHOST STORY

I've found three people now who claim they've seen
the girl's ghost underneath the apple tree
where she last met her lover on the night
he strangled her. Sue is upset with me:
she says things need repair around the house;
a grown man shouldn't waste his time asking
about ghosts. You know, Mom, that I don't believe
in ghosts, but she's become a legend here;
her murder gave the farmers something besides
planting to talk about. As you'd expect,
the girl was beautiful—with straight, black hair
that caught the moonlight like a summer lake;
astonished, dark-brown eyes; and skin so pale
some people wondered if she might be ill.
But no one could describe the boy, except
he lisped. The girl was pregnant when she died,
and everyone is sure he murdered her,
although he disappeared from town without
a fingerprint to make it certain he
was *there* that night. Her being pregnant doesn't
seem to me sufficient proof, and yet
it's also said the boy refused to help
his father with the milking chores. Three nights
I hid behind the old, stone orchard wall
to watch the apple tree, not expecting
truly to see her ghost, yet trying to
imagine her actually as she stood
there waiting for her lover to appear.
The third night someone came—a man, I'd say
about my height and build, and carrying
a stick or rifle, maybe hunting for
raccoons; or else her sleepless father might
have wandered through the orchard wishing
to outwalk his grief. I called to him. At first,
as if expecting me, he looked around,

then ran across the orchard to the woods.
Sue says I'm lucky that he didn't shoot.
          Sue doesn't know I've come to talk to you.
The difference between Dad's books and what
the farmers saw is only that Dad knows
his characters exist as words. Explain
to Sue all *his* inventions are just ghosts!
And yet I wanted Sue to understand
the real fear that girl felt. Picture her face!—
that's what I should have said-surely someone
might have perceived the danger she was in
and tried to rescue her. That's what her father
should have done—or else some neighbor's boy
who loved her, though she had rejected him.
And if I write her history, at least
her memory will live—if not her child.
          I'll get the details right—the scudding clouds,
the apple trees in rows, a piled stone wall,
the lacy, sleeveless dress that showed her arms.
But whom should I include—her father, Sue,
both you and Dad, a neighbor's boy, myself?
Sue's almost got to see her underneath
the apple tree in August moonlight, fear
on her hushed face, the shaded flowing
of her silver arms, a cameo around
her thin, tense throat, maybe just like the one
you always wear, engraved with circling whales,
that has my tinted portrait tucked inside.

COINCIDENCE

Don't be alarmed! Let me sit here with you
to watch the waterfall. It may sound like
I'm telling you a tale, but listen, please,
then maybe you'll believe that I'm sincere,
and this coincidence, finding you here
beside this rocky pool, leaning against
this ancient tree with evening light reflecting
off the water on your face as if
you were the image of the waterfall,
may have some special meaning for us both.
    I met a girl, a year ago, sitting
where you sit now, her chin upon one knee,
like a statue, arms wrapped around her legs.
I told her she reminded me of someone
I once loved who died within her sleep.
She let me talk and liked my company,
and seemed to understand my grief as if
it were her own. I could have sworn her eyes
were moist when speckled light reflected on them
from the waterfall. She lived at home
out by the bay, but worked not far from me,
and she agreed to meet for lunch next week
by the stone lion at the library.
    I waited angry for an hour, fearing
someone had pushed her on the subway tracks.
Maybe she got the date wrong; maybe she too
had waited, felt abandoned, and gone home?
How could I know? And then I realized
I wasn't certain that I knew her name.
Laurel, had she said Laurel? I wasn't sure.
Could Laurel be her last name? What had I
to go on otherwise? And so I called
the Laurels listed in the Bayside phone book—
five every night. The tenth try that I made
brought me her voice in a subdued "Hello"
that seemed to echo from some distant cave.

One second I was sure, but then she said:
"There's no Miss Laurel here." I realized,
abashed, I knew the voice-I must have called
my mother's house. Pretending innocence,
I said, "Excuse me, please." and left the phone,
wondering if she knew that it was me.
            Having run out of Laurels, I then tried
some other names of other plants or flowers,
randomly selected, for I figured
coincidence was now my only hope.
And yet I always asked, "Is Laurel home?"
One night a voice replied, "Miss Laurel died
over a year ago." I hung up trembling,
never made another call. But then
I dreamed Laurel sat by the pond where first
I saw her just as you sit now. Slowly,
as if floating step by nearing step
along the mossy path, I reached to touch her
when she turned to me and raised her arms.
Her eyes and mouth were blurred—as if reflected
upon water, moving as the water moved,
murmuring, but not with words. A lion
resting on a rock, guarding his high cave,
nodded: *if I returned I'd find you here.*
            I knew I'd see the pond-light on your face;
I knew the waterfall along the stones
would echo human sounds—calling sounds
and pleasure sounds. I'm sure I've seen that lion's
look of sorrow on your face before.
Can you believe me though you may suspect
I've read this story somewhere in a book?
While this light lasts, maybe you'll let me touch
your lips, and then you'll tell me who *you* are.

SECRETS

I doubt that you remember her—except
that final summer when we took the house
beside the bay. I vowed to wait until
right now to tell you how your mother died.
Do you still have her photograph—the one
in which her hands are cupped, with you trying
to peek inside? Every morning even
before I woke, she took you for a walk
to search for starfish scattered on the beach.
You were excited after you returned,
but then you'd sink into a sudden gloom
without a cause that I could see; you'd go
into your room and sit there with your shells,
arranging them in boxes; you'd stay inside
all afternoon. At night your mother talked
about your moods, though in your room, I thought,
when playing with your shells, you seemed content.
        You had one smooth quartz stone, your favorite,
and every time we looked you had it placed
inside another box. A thousand times
your mother asked me what I thought that meant.
I thought the stone meant you; the boxes meant
your made-up lives. Your mother thought the stone
was her—that you were putting her away—
but never told you what she guessed. Claiming
they were all beautiful, especially
the rounded stone, you scared us when you said
it was the only one that had itself
inside itself. The way your mouth was fixed
warned us to inquire no more. Your mother
wept all night; we held each other, kissing
gently in the dark, though something private
deep in her sobbing tightened her. She said:
"I don't know why I haven't done things right."

I promised her we'd take a trip, and when
her spirits rose, it seemed to me that you
no longer switched the stone from box to box.
We flew down to Bermuda where we took
a cabin by the beach. At night we strolled
the curving shore, collecting colored stones
and seashells to bring home, or curled together,
hugging, naming whatever stars we knew.
She told me things I'd never heard—like once
her mother ran off with her father's friend.
One moonlit evening we undressed each other
on the beach to take a swim. We raced
into the water, holding hands, and then
I let her go so I could watch. Flawless
as polished marble, oh her smooth arms gleamed,
plunging like dolphins as she dove; wind gusts
blew clouds across the moon, and she was gone.
        "Didn't you search for her?" the captain asked,
"Couldn't she swim?" "The water was so dark,"
I said, "and yes, she grew up by the sea."
"Was she depressed?" he asked, and I assured him
she was never happier. "Strange tides,"
I thought I heard him say. Sometimes I dream
that she gets washed up farther down the beach,
having forgotten who she is and who
we are, and that she is alive, living
another life. And then I am awake,
wishing something familiar—like the feel
of stone—might bring her back to us. We must
forget the past; we have a new life now.
Alice loves you—she's all you really know
since she moved in with us. Can you recall
your clinging to her on our wedding day,
helping her unpack? You kept the picture
of her sitting on her mother's lap.
        I didn't tell you how your mother died
because so much remained unknown. Promise

never to tell Alice—she's heard enough.
This has to be *our* secret; promise me.
This little golden starfish—take it, Joan—
I've saved it for the necklace that I gave you
when you turned thirteen; your mother bought it
by herself the day before she died.
She said that having secrets was her way
of holding on, and that you'd understand.

SISTER TO BROTHER

Look, there it is—I'm sure that is the oak
we built our tree house in the final summer
Grandpa was alive. The tree house that
you built might be more accurate; you never
let me hammer; passing nails was my job.
        Thanks for not asking why I brought you here;
maybe as my brother you can sense
what's troubling me. Those summers on the farm—
we were close then, with Grandma watching us:
"You've got to take your sister," she would say,
"a family is like a hand—fingers
are useless one by one." Sit here with me
beneath the oak, I want to try to talk.
        I haven't been myself—I'm pregnant and
I don't know if the father's John or Bill.
I thought I'd better wait to choose which one
to marry until I slept with both, and now,
whichever one I choose, it would be like
marrying two men; the other's ghost
would be there in my bed—and in my child.
        I'm thinking of not keeping it—it's still
only a little hungry speck of cells.
Should I discuss this with both John and Bill?
And what if one says, "Yes:' the other "No"?
Last week, when I had lunch with Dad, I felt
I'd lost hold of myself. He was about
to pay the bill when suddenly he looked
much younger than he's looked in years—his face
seemed smooth, his nose more aquiline, like yours,
his lips more curved and tilting to the left.
And then I thought: "My God, what if he's not
my father after all?" Now do you see?—
I've lost my sense of what it's safe to trust.
        It's crazy, but the hardest thing for me
to talk about is that I feel it's you
who are to blame for this. Remember how

you made me bait your hooks when we hiked down
to fish in Grandpa's pond for perch and bass?
They'd wriggle to get free; how could they know
that it was not my fault? I still can't stand
the taste of fish, the crumbly meat. Sometimes
I'd sneak down to the tree house by myself
and make believe you'd gone off on a trip;
I wrote the letters that you sent to me.
Then Grandpa left and died away from home,
and Grandma wouldn't talk of him. She'd weave
until the window light would fade, and say:
"This is the best work that I've ever done."
　　　　How did you get her tapestry from Dad?
Dad always claimed that it belonged to him.
But Grandma liked to weave things in for us:
I'm sure that tall oak in the woods behind
the farmhouse is our tree, and those white specks,
like trickled light among the round leaves,
maybe they're you and me. You should have told me
Grandpa left to die; he was afraid
we'd see him broken at the end. And yet
what I suspected was much worse. Always
something's missing that I need to know.
　　　　After the farm was sold, you didn't seem
to care for me as much, or notice me,
and it's been years since I've asked for your help.
After my lunch with Dad, that whirling night,
still feeling that I couldn't trust myself
and therefore couldn't keep the child, I dreamed
I pulled a baby out of Grandpa's pond;
it had your face. It stood up, waved good-bye,
and walked away into the yellow house
of Grandma's tapestry. Maybe the reason
I can't decide is that I never knew
whether you *had* to love me-was it me?—
or was it love for Grandma's sake? That's what
I mean, there's always something I don't know!
　　　　What difference can it make to you to know

who my child's father is? I'm sure, if you
adopted it, Grandma's ghost would say:
"I'll weave it into my next tapestry;
a family must hold together like
a hand." Then I could try to start again.
Just ask your wife, I know she'll understand;
some women can't have children of their own.

TRYING TO SEPARATE

Please give me room, Howard! I've tried before
to tell you this—I have to leave you, oh
that came out wrong, there's no way I can find
the words that sound as if I'm making sense.
Not *you,* Howard, it isn't *you* I'm leaving,
it's Vermont, the starving deer, the spring
that never comes, the gloomy ice and clay.
Even when late sun lingers in the birches,
darkness fills my mind. I need more light,
more red—not just a pair of cardinals,
but flocks of them. There's no red in the earth;
purple spreads in the mountains when the sun
descends behind the hemlock trees as if
the animals were grieving there. And fall
comes much too soon, the yellows are too brief;
I don't have time here to forget myself.
I want to go to Tucson where I lived
before my mother died, where stones are red,
the desert light *feels* red—a gradual,
slow, steady red. I need more time to dwell
on images I want to paint. Don't joke
again about my always *seeing red!*
You once said that my painting is the cause,
but that's not first; I need a different light
than you to *see,* and then the paintings come.
You need Vermont, you need an inward light;
you need the feeling that each day is hard.
Love cannot feed itself with love. We've tried.
Love needs something outside itself—children—
and we've delayed deciding that too long.
You said one only chooses children after
one has had them; then they become like *place,*
then they're the *given* like the landscape is.
You think there's got to be some deeper cause
for breaking up. I fear you may be right,
but I can't find that cause; Howard, believe me,

I've really looked. All that I know is red,
and you desire gray; punishing winter
is your season, white birches are your light.
You need Vermont to be yourself. You do!
         Don't try to comfort me; don't touch me now—
that makes me angry when I want to talk—
for then you'll have a reason I should stay.
You'll say: admit it's *me* you want to leave,
admit you're angry, that it's not because
you love the goddamn red; you'll say we have our sunsets
blazing on the snow, we have our fire at night,
as if I'll give in—as I always do.

THE CRACKED APPLE TREE

Right on that branch we saw the snowy owl
the one time it arrived from Canada.
Don't cut it down! I know it's past the age
for bearing useful fruit; it crowds the house
and darkens both the upstairs rooms, but we
have changed the place enough—the well is new,
the paneled walls, and all those shelves you built
are crammed with books. The day we bought the house
old Philip put it in your mind to clear
the trees that blocked the vista to the west:
"People like to fix things up themselves,"
was what he said, and yet we've left it there
for over twenty years, just as you've left
his broken harrow rusting in the field
as if it were a piece of sculpture, though
it's like the rib cage of a dinosaur.

Philip was *afraid* to cut it down;
he told me that he saw a girl's ghost there
whose lover murdered her when she got pregnant.
She lived down the road before this house
replaced the one that burned, and Philip said
that we can find a record of her death
somewhere in the local files. Last week
when you were pruning it, you left your sweater
hanging on a branch, and when I took my walk
beside the stream before I went to bed,
I saw it flutter in the moonlit breeze
and thought of Philip's story of the girl.

My father kept a bear's head in his den
over his desk: he teased me as a child,
pretending that the bear would talk to him.
I never found out if he shot the bear.

I know you like to watch that great stone ridge,
framed by the distant Adirondack range,
after the brittle leaves have fallen down.
I've seen you sit beside the window, staring

at the long striations—yellow, tan, and brown
turning to orange as the sun comes up—
as if you saw something you couldn't share.
I've warned the children not to bother you
when you take on that inward mood of yours.

What if a blizzard drives the snowy owl
down here again, and he can't find his branch?
What if the man returns, filled with remorse,
seeking his lover by our apple tree?
One can't be certain such things don't occur.
Your books are full of mysteries and puzzles,
half-invented memories, and choices
that can't be explained. You'll never know for sure
if Philip made the murder story up
about the pregnant girl as an excuse
to leave the tree uncut. You'll never know
if I invented father's talking bear.
I saw the look that crossed your face when I
told you about the girl; I'm certain you
were ready then to let me have my way.

You leave the harrow lying in the field;
you keep your thoughts about the layered ridge
and what its colored lines remind you of,
and let me keep the cracking apple tree
for our love's sake. For if you don't, my dear,
I'll put my wedding nightgown on and stand
there in the moonlight on the tree stump, still
as your ridge, as if I *were* a snowy owl.

TRYING TO RECONCILE

You shouldn't have gone off the pill without
your telling me! Even if we decide
to have the child now, even if it's mine,
it was your choice, so don't pretend your motive
was to help our marriage last. A prick
groping the dark for some anonymous
relief, that's all you wanted me to be,
that's all I am. If you believe a child
can bind our lives, allow me time to come
to feel that for myself. But it's control
you want—another way I'll need you and
you've got me then! I want a child to free
something in me more generous than sex
that brings me back to my own emptiness.
I've got to reach you, and I've got to try
to try, or else I'm only me again.
Maybe we've lived in this same house too long.
I see the same striations in the cliffs
emerging orange from the mist each dawn.
The short-eared owl—I've seen him sitting like
a glacier in the moonlit apple tree
a hundred times, the same ancestral grip
still holding him, the mouse limp in his beak,
always the victim with his testament
of blood upon the snow in March, and yet
without regret like you and me, breathing
our remorseful sleep, blaming each other
for what we lack ourselves. Maybe we need
enemies to injure, more loves to betray,
to learn those cosmic patterns of defeat—
like limestone fossils in our hearth. I could
read pity there if we asked less of love
to rescue us from being what we are.

Watching the stars, pity is what I feel
for all of us, gaping with thoughts of leaving
our own lives, banished even from ourselves
like stars receding with their reddened speed.
Will they come hurtling back, explode, and start the whole
damned thing again? I'll rant my way
back to my life—at least that's better than
accusing you of your own emptiness.
      It eases me to watch the whipping snow
piling against the trees to starve the deer
who die without a plea in their white minds
for help to come. "Hidden death" you called the pill
"refusing to accept we'll be replaced."
It's like my fantasy of strangling you—
as if to take a life could save my own.
Look there by the gully—it's the lame fox
whose broken leg we set last summer when
he was abandoned as a cub, staring
at us with his black eyes. Is there a chance
that he remembers us? "An empty casket
a life should be," those were your words
that made me *taste* the pill. I'm listening,
to feel your thoughts as if I touched
my own, as if your choice were in my groin.
      "Someone's got to help that wounded fox,"
you said, "since its own mother won't:' "That's not
the way that Nature works," was my reply:
"now she's forgotten it's alive." You know
I'll love the child. You know I know it's mine,
don't you? I have no choice except to choose—
choose something or we're all just whirling stars,
just snow the blind wind heaps upon the snow.

TRILLIUM

Maybe I shouldn't tell you this—you are
his daughter, Beth, as much as you are mine—
I think your father's having an affair.
Last spring he started hiking in the woods,
just as he used to do when you were born;
he said he needed time to be alone.
But then I noticed he began to mention
subtle things about the flowers—details.
"Everything about the trillium comes
in threes," he said, "petals, sepals, stigmas;
the ovate leaves, all three of them, whorl right
below the triple shining crimson flowers."
He'd follow me around the house, describing
what he'd seen, and get annoyed with me
if I did not respond enough. Last week
I couldn't help myself; I blurted out:
"What *do* you want to say to me?" I see
you're skeptical, and yet you know your father
well enough to sense when he is holding
something back. Why should the fact a flower
has suggestive names—like wake-robin,
stinking benjamin, wet-dog trillium—
be so significant to him, unless
there's a confession in those names, hiding
even from himself? He says wake-robin
is its name because it blossoms just as
. spring arrives. I think he feels that spring
can come again for him. At our age, Beth,
men often have the need to start again,
and you'd be wrong to think your father's not
like other men. You love the wilderness
and gardening; you know the wild flowers' names
and when to plant the lettuce and the peas.
Why can't he take you sometimes on his walks?

I figured you'd get angry if I spoke
what's really on my mind, Lately you have
so little patience when I try to share
my thoughts with you—as if our being close
threatens your sense of who you are. I'm sure
you know that stinking benjamin describes
the odor of the trillium—it's like
a sweating body, a body dying
or making love is what he didn't say.
I'm asking only for your empathy,
not condemnation of his so-called walks.
No daughter ever loved herself unless
she loved her mother also. Beth, I'm scared,
I don't know how to meet this need of his,
and I'm too old to start again—not old,
but old enough to want to keep the loves
I've built upon: his love, my dear, and yours.
And his remaining here gives both of us
the needed distance it's so good to cross.
        Remember how the two of us would bake
his birthday cake? I'd let you split the eggs,
and you'd sit on the kitchen counter, spreading
thick brown fudge in swirls, touching my lips
with one delicious finger. You believe
all this is fantasy—that father's walks
are innocent? What has he said to you?
I think you're keeping something to yourself.
        When you were in my womb, you'd press your head
against the pulsing of my artery.
You were the hardest child to get to bed,
and when from sheer exhaustion you let go,
your lips would tighten and expose your teeth,
your mouth turn downward with a little drool;
I'd stand there looking baffled by such sleep.
        Is there a chance he'll leave me for this *girl*?
What do you think? We haven't talked like this

in years—about the birds and flowers, no less!
We make a funny triangle: husband,
wife, and trillium—'till trillium do
us part. Thanks for the smile—I need it now,
and promise not to ask what else you know
about my rival, wet-dog trillium!

LEVIATHAN

You've kept your word and come to visit me.
You know how much I love this house, although
I'm lonely here. Your father used to walk
this beach with me, then sit on that smoothed rock—
as if the sea prepared a seat for him—
observing sails tack past the buoy bells,
waiting for a whale's spout to appear.
It seemed he would forget how many times
he told me: when he was a boy, he took
his rowboat out to get a close look at
the baby whale that strayed into the bay.
Descending underneath your father's boat,
it surged up bubbling on the other side,
flipped around, dove beneath his boat again,
drenching your father with each salty plunge.
Circling beyond the reef, its parents flung
their thirty tons into the sky—with a
vast whoosh of blown-out sea, their plume of spray,
and then a hiss of air as if it sucked
the whole horizon in—displaying white
repeating patterns on their undersides,
pounding their tails to summon its return.
Your father claimed it dove beneath his boat
at least a dozen times before it left,
but he regretted that he didn't leap
into the sea himself to play with it.
I'm still amazed to think how all his life
that rankled him, and yet that may have been
the most ecstatic day he ever spent.
"I swear the damn thing laughed at me," he'd say,
"its whistles, chirps, and clicks composed a song."
Your father thought he was a happy man,
but something willed about his happiness
showed through, something deliberate. I felt
he had to make a choice to hold gloom down.
And yet he couldn't bring himself to say

what troubled him; I don't know if he knew,
and never did find out. A certain blank,
distracted gaze would sweep across his face
when that grim mood of his came on, making
his eyes seem vague—the way a camera
blurs one's age-lines when it's not in focus.
Sadness in him—if it is accurate
even to say that it was *his*—rarely
connected with particular events;
it simply would emerge and disappear
like hemlocks in the autumn morning mist,
and there was nothing I could do to help.
I had to live with it, so I assumed
that I was not the cause. Last night you spoke
to me in that remote, abstracted voice
your father sometimes used, when you remarked:
"There's just one man my wife would leave me for—
our son; it's like competing with a ghost."

      Your father used to praise me for the care
I'd given you and Jennifer, but not
the caring I showed him. I don't mean he
would blame me for his sorrow, yet I'm sure
he wished somehow I could have found a way
to lighten what he called the tears of things.
How could I? What he felt was much too deep
and too impersonal—like rain, or mist,
or snowfall in the oak's remaining leaves.
I fear he passed that sorrow on to you.
Yes, he was right about himself—sorrow
revealed the soul of things, especially
when they were beautiful; sorrow for him
was out there moving in the universe.

      Perhaps he loved the changes of the fall
too much: the orange maples, goldenrod
at the field's edge, and you, your muscled arms
just like his own. Before you left, you split
the last dry cord of wood for him. He leaned
against the window watching you, and when

you came inside—do you recall?—he told
his story of the baby humpback whale,
but with a change. I'd never heard before
that when the whales dive down and disappear,
they leave patches of oily water, almost
imperceptible and strangely still,
which look like human footprints on the sea.

REMAINS

My ship departs next Saturday. Ruth knows
I have to go. This time, Dad, keep in touch.
We'll study whales, both stranded and alive:
their great intelligence, how they maintain
communication over distances
with sonic pictures showing what they feel
from sounds produced—they have no vocal cords—
within their lungs. Think of it, Dad, pictures
of what they feel from sequences of clicks!
Their brains are larger than a man's; the links
connecting stimuli to response are
inexhaustible; their memories possess
a power we can barely comprehend.
Professor Singer says they demonstrate
a vast capacity to show affection.
Tell Mom that Ruth and I have broken up;
I'll write to her. Mom warned me once that Ruth
could not accept my love because Ruth feels
she isn't worthy to be loved. And now
I'm not sure what remains to be explained.
Ruth kept accusing me—though it's not true—
of loving someone else, and yet perhaps
I did hold something back. She'd say: 'All you
talk about is whales." But we're killing them!
A hundred tons of pain with each harpoon!
Millions of years evolved what Cousteau calls
"extraordinary gentleness." No whale
will hurt a diver if he's not attacked,
and yet we're killing them! The great blue whale's
almost extinct. I can't accept a future
with no whales remaining in the sea,
but Ruth won't get involved, although she knows
what sorrow is. And if I write to Mom
to say I've got to help the whales, she'll think
that's *my* excuse for leaving Ruth. Not so.

Our species can't embrace our mortal lives,
and killing makes us feel omnipotent.
        The twenty-pound harpoon grenade explodes
inside their flesh. Reports describe their cry—
part howl, part plea; they dive down, opening
the hooks which gouge their organs out. They're dragged
back bobbing to the ship. The sea swirls red;
the air takes on a fiery haze. You know
the whale is dead when its gigantic mouth
opens as if it were about to speak.
A whale will swim between an injured whale
and the harpooning ship; or if he's hurt
and has become a burden to the herd,
he may decide to stop his breath and die.
It's difficult for whales to mate because
they're too huge to plunge in like simians;
there's pain in their repeated, strained attempts.
Whales breathe like us, so they must rise and sink
together as they try to merge, using
their flippers to embrace each other's bulk.
Often the sea clouds with defeated sperm.
Gray whales require a second male to help,
to lie across the coupling pair so they
can keep their balance in the churning sea.
Ruth wonders how they've managed to survive
through the millennia. Mom thinks such mating
shows they are incapable of love.
        You've got to hear the whales sing, hundreds
with modulating voices: mewings, trills,
janglings and whoops, creakings and bellowings,
each making its own sounds for the sheer joy
of making sounds. Lagorio remarked,
"It's a cathedral in the sea!" We can't
explain those alternating calls, unless
they're joining with the family of whales.
When I left Ruth, I pictured you and Mom,
still young, in your first house, and lost myself

thinking that I was you, imagining
you could foresee you'd have *me* as your son.
The swaying bed became a whale, holding
me there, more buoyant than I'd ever felt,
and all the whales were singing, praising me.

PRAYER FOR PRAYER

Darling, splitting the wood can wait until
the wind dies down. I want to try to say
what's troubling me, although we vowed before
we married that we'd keep our own beliefs
and let the children choose. They've left home now;
there's not much more that we can do for them;
it's you and me together, only *us*,
and I'm afraid you won't get into heaven,
not having turned to God. Without you, how
could I be happy there, unless God wills
that I forget this life? I don't want that!
The March sun hasn't thawed those icicles
gleaming along the edges of our roof;
perhaps this constant wind has numbed my faith.

I've never had to ask you this before,
but would you try to pray? Make up the words
if only for my sake; start thanking God
for daily things like breakfast oranges
heaped in the yellow bowl your mother painted—
a couple bathing in a waterfall—
our wedding gift of thirty years ago;
thank Him for your routine: feeding the birds
in winter, pruning apple trees in spring;
thank Him for splitting wood. You know I know
that even when you grumble, still it's work
you love. Nothing I do will feel complete
until I've given thanks for doing it,
so that I'm not alone: like thanking you
for thanking me when I prepare a meal
adds grace to grace. That's not a phrase you'd use;
you would prefer to hold some meanings back:
"Grace is not fattening, how can it hurt?"
but what we feel is not so far apart,
though maybe it's the very space God wants
to test us with? My mother used to say:

"You cannot cling to what you love with all
your strength; God made some special part of us
for letting go." I understood her when
our children left, and I can almost hear
the spaces where they were. Maybe sorrow
is allowed in heaven, so God won't have to
cancel human love by making us forget?
        I won't forget, not willingly; one day
in paradise, watching the clouds, I'd think
of you standing beside the frozen stream,
eyeing the wood still to be split and stacked,
and I'd be back on earth—at least at heart.
God means for marriages to end with death,
but after that the Bible isn't clear.
Perhaps God's love begins where human love
completes itself, and yet I'll never tire
of the past we've shared. I know you'll promise me
you'll try to pray, and then you'll ask the Lord
to help me find the strength to give up prayer-
as if God would enjoy your joke; you'll swear:
"By yonder icicle, I'll love the world until
it does me in!" Thinking is the problem;
we can't escape the sorrow of an end
without an end, death going on and on.
Although you never speak of it, I know
your father died while he was splitting wood;
your mother's telling always starts the same:
"Some snow had fallen on his knitted hat,"
as if for her all time had stopped. Maybe
that is what heaven's like? She seems to smile,
but then the age-lines darken in her face
        Darling, I know you know something in me
approves your laughing at my need to pray.
By yonder icicle, what human love
allows, we have! But don't stand grinning with
that orange in your mouth as if you were
some sacrificial pig! Go split more wood

while I put dinner on; listen to God's
silences even as the wind blows through
the icicles and piles snow by our shed;
we may be in for quite a night of it.

FROM
Clayfeld Rejoices,
Clayfeld Laaments
(1987)

CLAYFELD'S MICROSCOPE

Clayfeld recalls his hobby as a boy:
    cultivating protozoa
in water taken from the tadpole pond
    behind the barn.
Peering through his birthday microscope,
    he watches an amoeba
plump out its pseudopod, engulf some algae,
    meditate a moment,
then constricting in the middle
    by sheer force of will,
just pull apart, tearing in two its body,
    nucleus and all.
Once Clayfeld sat for five hours straight
    to see how many times
the first amoeba would divide, straining
    not to lose sight of it.
He named her Mom so he could follow her
    among the swarming
paramecia, euglena, dead specks,
    and bits of stone.
A problem there, of course, since once
    Mom had divided,
which one then was Mom? "How can you tell?"
    Clayfeld's twin brother asked,
yet Clayfeld had the spooky sense
    somehow he knew—
something about the way Mom moved,
    some fluid ease,
enabled him to choose which one she was.
    Clayfeld was not as certain
of the girls at school. It puzzled him
    to find how rapidly
his feelings changed, how none of them
    attracted him for long,
though he'd still tighten in his pants
    when they were giggling

in the library, or when they
    globbed together
in the cafeteria. One day,
    sitting with them
during lunch, Mima, the girl he liked
    about a month ago,
stuffed both her cheeks with gooey bread,
    puckered her lips,
and blew a slimy kiss at him. But something
    crazy happened when
he squinted back his eyes: he saw
    her face as if she were
a huge amoeba, her dark mouth its nucleus,
    the instant it divides,
and screamed at her, "Don't do that, Mom!"
    Their laughter made him blush
so hard he burst into another of his
    periodic nosebleeds;
they had to lead him, wadded napkins
    covering his cheeks,
to get an ice pack from the skinny nurse:
    "Old Bones will save you!"
taunted through the corridors. Clayfeld
    got Mirna pregnant when he
turned eighteen. Through the cold night before
    they went to the abortionist,
with money borrowed from his older sister,
    they made such compulsive love
beside the dry stone wall his father built
    to frame the barn that they amazed
themselves. Their bodies seemed beyond whatever words
    might bring them back to who they were.
"Look at the stars; I've never seen so many
    scattered stars!" was all
Clayfeld could say. Mirna wept to herself
    as dawn stirred in the pines.
"I'm sorry for us all," he thought she murmured,
    swearing that he'd marry her

when they were old enough to keep a child.
    Morosely kissing her good-bye
before she climbed the ramp to fly to college
    in the west, Clayfeld did not admit
as their lips parted that he felt relieved.
    For one whole week he stared
into his microscope, but when a cell
    divided, Clayfeld now could not
distinguish which one was the one
    he started with, and when
the time arrived for him to go, he left a note
    that turned his ordinary
microscope into a gift he hoped
    his brother might enjoy:
"For me it's been like studying the universe."
    At school his interests changed to how
the earth evolved; Clayfeld became a sculptor
    when his gloom got worse.

CLAYFELD'S DUCK

Clayfeld's father died after two strokes
    when Clayfeld was fifteen.
His last words were: "Take care of Buff,"
    but Clayfeld didn't know
anyone named Buff, and wondered
    whether Buff might have been
his father's dog when he was young. His mother,
    one year later, married Bill,
so all of them moved north to Maine,
    making the cattle farm their home
where Bill's pa had been born. Bill bought some ducks,
    plump, luminescent white
with orange bills, and Clayfeld kept them
    in the unused chicken coop
that he repaired. Six eggs appeared;
    Clayfeld inspected them
each morning when he did his chores,
    freshening the water for his ducks,
bringing them their grain. One night a weasel
    broke into their pen;
when Clayfeld found them, feathers fluttered
    in the dusty air, although
they had survived, quivering together
    in the corner of their hutch.
The eggs were shattered—all but one
    which had a jagged crack-line
like a pumpkin's grin. As Clayfeld poked it
    gently in the gusting dawn,
a head popped out as if it were a toy,
    and Clayfeld jumped,
gashing his head against the gate.
    Some birds know who their mother is
because mother means the first thing moving
    that her baby sees; and, yes,
you've guessed it, that's what Clayfeld was:
    fate had inscrutably decreed

that Clayfeld would become a mother duck.
  Ishmael scuttled after him,
as ducks always have done, and squawked
  if Clayfeld walked too far ahead.
At dinnertime, Clayfeld would put him
  in the pocket of his shirt
against his chest and let him snuggle in.
  His sister scolded him
for interfering with the course of things,
  and yet she helped him build a box,
set with a bulb, to warm his duck at night.
  Bill lost his hand
trying to fix a combine in the field,
  and carried it a hundred yards,
wrapped tightly in his shirt, back to the house.
  When Ishmael was full grown,
Clayfeld released him on the lake
  to join the other ducks
as maple leaves were falling and red squirrels
  rasped at each other
in the chill of sharpened light. In June
  Clayfeld returned from school,
and there was Ishmael in the lake as if
  awaiting him. Clayfeld hooted,
flapping his arms, but Ishmael would not
  come to him, coasting along
the hazy water's farthest edge.
  Bill had been fitted
with a plastic hand, and Clayfeld was surprised
  that he could cut his food
or pull the trigger of his gun, but when
  his mother pressed it to her lips
to show how proud she was of Bill,
  the shattered eggs, the hunchbacked weasel
still surveying them, flashed in his mind.
  For one whole month Clayfeld
glutted himself with food, or sitting silent
  on the limestone ledge, he'd watch

the ducks paddling around the lily pads.
  Bill kneeled beside him,
resting his plastic hand on Clayfeld's arm;
  "Isn't that Ishmael," Bill asked,
"the third one in formation by the cove?
  A stranger couldn't tell him from the rest,"
Clayfeld surprised himself to hear what words
  leaped out of him: "Ishmael's the one
beyond that bank of stones;' he said, knowing
  a grove of birches was reflected
in the water there, reflecting in the sun.

CLAYFELD'S GLOVE

Clayfeld believed indulging in one's whims
    improved the circulation—
of despondent blood; whims, the sculptor in him
    could persuade himself,
counted as a form of inspiration.
    One day, browsing
in a sports equipment store, he noticed how
    the baseball gloves had changed,
how large the webbing had become, and he decided
    he would fly to Arizona,
where his mother lived, to see if she had stored
    the yellow baseball glove
Clayfeld had oiled and pounded into shape
    when he was still a boy.
"Are you all right?" the salesman asked,
    and Clayfeld knew
he must have blushed to recollect the time
    he'd grabbed his baseball glove
to hide his private parts that night
    his mother, without warning,
walked into his room. He thought maybe he'd sculpt
    a naked statue of himself-
a true artistic first: a baseball glove where once
    a fig leaf would have been.
Clayfeld awoke in Arizona to the smell
    of lamb chops sizzling,
which his mother served him with his eggs,
    just as she used to do
when he was lifting weights to put some muscle
    on his skinny frame.
"Everything I've kept of yours," she said,
    "is packed away in boxes
chronologically and stacked in the garage."
    Shoes, hair clippings, letters,
layer after layer, like excavations
    from an ancient Jericho,

waited to be exhumed. And then, behold!
    he found a baseball glove,
but one too skimpy to have been his own.
    Maybe, he thought, this was
his father's glove; maybe Mother had mistaken
    Father's glove for his?
Another statue he might sculpt appeared
    in Clayfeld's mind: his father, poised
in naked grandeur, just as Michelangelo
    had once conceived his David,
slingshot stone in hand, prepared to backhand
    any well-hit grounder
that might yield the rally-killing double play.
    "I don't know how
this glove could be your father's,"
    Clayfeld's mother scolded him,
and then it all came swirling back to her:
    "You couldn't have been more
than four or five," she said, "that spring your father
    took you out to have a catch
when he had finished with his chores—and 1
    mean every single day!
I'd stand there in the doorway shouting
    "Dinner will get spoiled
unless the two of you come in right now!"
    but nothing I could threaten
seemed to do much good. And so one evening
    after you had muddied up
the living room as usual, I boiled the glove,
    piled mashed potatoes
neatly in the pocket, sprinkled it
    with parsley, squeezed into
my tightest bathing suit, my highest heels,
    and sashayed in
to score my point." A statue of his mother
    formed in Clayfeld's mind,
and then Clayfeld recalled his father's words
    before he tucked him

into bed that night. "From now on, Son,
    we'll have to end
our catch on time." It had begun to rain.
    He saw the red buds
of the maple tree outside his room
    begin to sway and swell.
His father handed him a sandwich
    he had sneaked upstairs
inside his baseball cap. "I'll bet you didn't know
    that I could cook," he said.
Now in this Arizona noon, those open boxes
    blazing in the entryway
of the garage, the lines in Clayfeld's mother's face
    seemed smoothed out by the sun.
"Yes, everything will be put back exactly
    in its place;' he promised her.
But Clayfeld wondered if his grief would ever end.
    Maybe if he had children
of his own? He thought someday he'd do
    his father's bust—he'd catch the grim
thrust of his head, like David looking past his shoulder
    through the empty light,
without his body there to trouble him.

CLAYFELD'S OPERATIC DEBUT

Clayfeld considered Rita the most gifted student
    he had taught in years
at Greensville University where Clayfeld's
    basic sculpture course
in structure and material was famous
    in the dorms as Bones and Stones.
"You have the touch," Clayfeld assured her
    when her confidence was down
one sleeting afternoon as they were in his studio
    discussing her rough sketches
for a life-size sculpture of herself.
    Tears came to Rita's eyes;
"I only told him that his student singers
    are inspired by him," she said,
"and then Professor Hornblow propositioned me."
    Fire springing to his cheeks,
Clayfeld cried out, "My God, he's older than I am!"
    Professor Hornblow was contrite
when Clayfeld icily confronted him, pleading
    he would reform if Clayfeld promised
not to file a sexual harassment charge.
    "I've suffered punishment enough,"
he said, "just knowing what I know about myself."
    To his surprise, Clayfeld then swore
he would say nothing to the dean if Hornblow
    offered him the part
of Mephistopheles in *Faust* to be premiered
    at Greensville in the spring.
"I know the role by heart," Clayfeld, amused,
    could hear himself proclaim, and so
the two of them shook hands to seal the compact
    that began their partnership.
Clayfeld's interpretation of the character
    was that, no less than aged Faust,
desire for lasting youth consumed the Devil's heart;
    desire for more desire

had poisoned Satan's love for endless love
        into its jealous opposite.
Clayfeld on stage would stare past Faust,
        twirling his waxed mustachios,
flashing his *you-must-pay-the-rent* wide grin
        at every woman in his view—
each face, he thought, was beautiful if ever
        he could know her well enough—
but sympathetic longing swelled so thick
        in Clayfeld's throat,
his throbbing voice took on a dark vibrato
        trembling from his bones,
that vindicated Hornblow's bargain giving him
        the chance to sing the part.
"We all contain a world of hidden selves
        demanding birth; the sculptor must
release them into light," Clayfeld espoused
        to Rita much more formally
than he had planned, stiffly hugging her farewell
        that humid graduation day.
"I hope in time you will be proud of what
        I've learned from you," she said,
and vanished with her parents in the crowd.
        "A chauvinist Pygmalion
is what I am," Clayfeld tried to cheer himself,
        but he remained dejected, working
through the summer on a statue of his daughter
        sitting on a rock, her weight
thrown back upon her thin, unsteady arms,
        her face upturned to catch the sun.
"Her features could be anyone's," hissed Clayfeld to himself
        as Hornblow's tenor voice
accompanied his knocking at the door
        of Clayfeld's dusty studio.
"*Me voici!*" Clayfeld mellifluously greeted him
        as usual with mockery.
But fleshier than he remembered her, a shawl
        around her belly and her shoulders

like a hunched owl's wings disturbed for flight,
        Rita appeared at Hornblow's side:
"We wanted you to be the first to know;
        we ask your blessing," Rita said.
Clayfeld could not complete the statue
        of his daughter, though he tried
until October when the flailing trees,
        ablaze, revealed their branches
to the wind, and Clayfeld then decided with relief
        that he, as Mephistopheles,
cast out and wailing on the earth, at best could ease
        his own disfigured mind
by leaving her still struggling to find shape, and bent,
        just like the twisted slaves
of Michelangelo, who, pushing out in labor from
        confining stone, needing to laugh
or groan or sing, seem puzzled to be leaving home,
        their first, white, silent element.

CLAYFELD AMONG THE QUARKS

Physicists speak of the flavor of the quarks
when making the distinction between "u" and "d"
quarks . . . Color simply refers to an intrinsic.
property of the particles, just as electrical
charge and strangeness do . . . There are other
chargelike attributes carried by elementary
particles besides the familiar electrical one . . .
called strangeness, charm, beauty, and truth.

—JAMES S. TREFIL

Clayfeld sat up in bed at 3:00 A.M.,
     put on his baseball cap,
and woke his wife. Tears, truthful and delirious,
     slid to the crevices
around his lips. "The dinosaurs are dead—
     the latest theory claims a comet
hit the earth and raised a cloud of dust so huge
     the photosynthesizing sun
could not sustain the plants they ate," dark Clayfeld said.
     "I never meant to keep
their disappearance secret," Evelyn replied
     from underneath her pillow;
"really, dear, I would have told you if
     I hadn't known you knew."
"But did you also know our sun has used up
     half its hydrogen?
In just five billion years it will burn out."
     "Sweetheart, go back to sleep,
I promise that the sun will show its face tomorrow
     when the birds greet you,
our Vermont St. Francis, at their feeding place."
     Still Clayfeld couldn't rest:
"We've got to figure out how much material
     the universe contains—
it's like the question whether God exists—
     for if there's mass enough,

someday the stars will hurtle back,
    the *red shift* will reverse to blue,
and finally all matter will implode
    in one *big crunch* just like
the *big bang* fifteen billion years before,
    and start the universe anew.
I grieve to think of galaxies forever
    thinning out until there's nothing
but undifferentiated radiation
    without force to charm
chance into brewing up the soup of life."
    Yet Evelyn fed Clayfeld
bacon in the morning, cheerful, though complaining fat
    would cause his long-expected
heart attack. But Clayfeld persevered, the flavor
    of the smoky salt inspired
his tongue to savor all the spice
    of cherishing his death as if
mortality had been *his* choice, although
    the strangeness of familiar fear
returned when evening snowfall blurred all color,
    whitening the air.
So Clayfeld called his bachelor brother
    in Los Angeles, a physicist
whose work on quarks had helped trace back
    the cosmic clock to right
within a millisecond of the *big bang* that
    for Clayfeld meant: *Let there be light!*
"No one has seen a quark," his brother said;
    "they're particles deduced
from how atomic matter first evolved.
    I'll visit you in May,
and I'll explain why physicists hypothesize
    the quarks with quirky names."
He didn't come, but on that day commemorating
    Clayfeld's having joined the vast,
spectacular parade to cosmic nothingness
    exactly fifty years ago,

a box arrived marked: HANDLE QUARKS WITH CARE!
    When Clayfeld yanked the cord,
he saw six sewn, blue, beatific smiles—
    that seemed to know of earth
all that one needs to know—on six white dolls
    his brother must have made,
which, Evelyn remarked, resembled plump amoebae
    linked together arm in arm.
Each wore a necklace that spelled out its name:
    first truth and BEAUTY, then came
FLAVOR, COLOR, STRANGENESS, CHARM.

CLAYFELD'S ANNIVERSARY SONG

When the evolutionary biologist J. B. S. Haldane
was asked about the nature of the creator, he replied:
"An inordinate fondness for beetles."

    There's no accounting for
one's taste in love, my dear, even with God.
    Some eighty-five percent
of all animal species comprise insects,
    with an inscrutable
preponderance of beetles! Although they seem
    grotesque to you and me
(stag males can kill with their huge mandibles
    or seize their choiceless mates)
yet there they are, Nature's elect display,
    with such variety
embellishing a single theme great Bach's
    imagination pales
by comparison. Having invaded
    on water, land, and air,
adorers of decay, some woo their mates
    by rubbing their own wings
to rough out strains of ragged melody,
    while some display their fire
(protected by an inner layer of cells
    so they won't burn themselves)
delighting in each other with abandon
    we can't emulate.
A quibble in the cosmic scheme of things,
    no doubt: Nature is not
concerned with individuals, even
    species are cast away—
tonnage of dinosaurs with just a little
    climate shift. Yet, life alone
is what God seems to care about—only
    ongoing life, trying
new forms for His vast, slapdash enterprise
    of changing things. Against

such precedent divine, what arrogance
    is human constancy—
rebellion in the most unnatural
    and prideful way of love
seeking to preserve the past. No wonder
    we're appalled by death,
ashamed of our own sweat, and endlessly
    examining ourselves.
What parents ever wished their child would be
    an evolutionary
breakthrough, rendering us obsolete?
    The quintessential prayer
that dwells in every human heart repeats:
    O *Lord, keep things the same;*
let me be me again in paradise,
    reading in my old chair .
or strolling through a grove of evergreens.
    I fear that we'll be viewed
by Him as undeserving of the life
    we've got, and punished, yet
no differently than other creatures are—
    we'll be forgotten too,
beetles and all. Who knows—perhaps someday
    He'll tire: "Enough!" He'll cry,
and start a list of everything He's done.
    And when He gets way back
to counting us, and pictures you again,
    just as I see you now—
watering the wilted fuscia hanging
    beside the limestone wall,
plucking the dead leaves from the zinnias—
    He'll think: "It's not their fault
they measured time in anniversaries
    as if their need for meaning
made me manifest in *their* intent;
    I burdened them with an
excessive will to live. But by my beard,
    my beetles were magnificent!"

FROM

Before It Vanishes

(1989)

☾

BIG BANG

The present view of the creation, the "standard big bang model,"
maintains that the entire universe originated in an enormous explosion.
All matter was once concentrated into a very confined region in
a primordial matter soup. This matter soup expanded rapidly—it
exploded. In so doing it cooled down, enabling nuclei, then atoms, and
finally much later galaxies, stars and planets to condense out of it. This
explosion is still going on today.

—HEINZ R. PAGELS, *The Cosmic Code*

If I had been, in the beginning, God
            brooding upon absence,
I might have pondered that if matter could be snatched
            from emptiness in an immense

            explosion, then allowed,
      with its expanding space, to cool—
            yes, that's the way to father
forth a universe! According to the rule

            (My favorite) of *entropy*
      increase I'd make time irreversible,
            measure it out, enabling
nuclei, then atoms, galaxies—the full,

            harmonious display
of stars and planets to condense into
            existence, always changing,
always entertaining Me with something new.

            And scattered randomly throughout
My galaxies, conditions surely would occur
            for oxygen and carbon
to combine, under an ordinary star, to stir

                inert cells to divide
and replicate themselves, and live, until
                evolving consciousness reveals
My thoughts as children who can share the thrill

of watching, bud by bud by leaf,
                sweet fruitful things unfold
and be—and be replaced in shifts of light
from green to red, from green to gold,

and red consumed in flourishing decay.
        I worry that their mortal wish
                for life to last will ruin
their moment of abundance in life's feast. . . . Relish

                it all, My sons, with eyes, with ears;
savor all songful matter with your tongue,
                like soup, with zestful words,
        and, while the universe is young—

just fifteen billion years, though colder now
                than when it was begun
blazing in hundred billions of degrees—
                this is *your* moment in the sun,

                a household star. Love her,
add laughter of your own to what you see:
                describe her as a grazing cow
across a field, perhaps a pollinating bee,

                who scents the blossoms
lifting upwind on the wafted air.
                Name her, Dolores, when she frowns
on cloudy afternoons, or, when her hair

is loose like flowing wheat,
praise her clear radiance and call her, Grace;
        don't let your knowledge—she
cannot remain—mar your approval of her face.

        And you, Professor Pagels,
you will serve as My new representative;
    of all the holy names I've had,
Big Bang is raunchy good as any you can give

        with My original
explosion, lo! still going on today . . .
    But please remind your rhyming friend
that even laughing fathers pass away.

AFTER ALL

After the first tenth of a second had passed, the universe cooled down
to about ten billion degrees Kelvin. . . . All that remained was electrons,
neutrinos, and photons. After three minutes had passed . . . the particles
were less agitated [and] the small contamination of protons and neutrons
[could] combine into nuclei. . . . Only after about a hundred thousand
years had elapsed did the temperature drop sufficiently for the electrons to
combine with the nuclei to form atoms. . . . After a few billion years, the
universe began to look as it presently does.

—HEINZ R. PAGELS, *The Cosmic Code*

I can recall my father telling me,
        while putting me to bed,
the story of God's first six days of work,
        before He rested, when He said:

"Let there be light," and, after He divided
waters of the deep with firmament,
"Let the dry land appear," was His command.
        I knew exactly what God meant

when He gave orders—things got done—unlike
        my father's threats to me
        that I had damn well better stop
pinching my brother. My dad just couldn't see

        that was impossible:
        so many pinchings back and forth required
two pinches more. In one way, though,
I knew they were alike: God never tired

        of saying certain words—"And let
the earth bring forth," when summoning the grass,
        or, when He made the stars—
"And let them be for signs." Dad couldn't pass

over those "Lets" without a rumble
in his voice, and then, for emphasis, each time
            "God saw that it was good"
came back, he'd jump up from my bed, and climb

        the box where my best toys were kept,
and launch his words out, rolling in the lull
            that marked the stages of God's work.
The word, "good," seemed too tame to me; "sensational,"

        is what I would have said,
"God saw it was sensational," the most
            complete world He could make;
maybe, I thought, God didn't want to boast,

        and, anyway, sensational
sounds funny to repeat, unlike plain "good."
            The fifth day was my favorite
                because I understood—

as if we shared a secret—why the Lord
            liked whales: they're big *and* friendly, though
they aren't fish, they're mammals—*that* is something,
            I believed, a god should know.

        Whales were the only creatures
God Himself had named; He should have made
            them on the same day He made men.
                Because I'm still afraid

        to let go in the dark, to sleep,
without a lullabying story saying how
                the universe began,
            Professor Pagels, tell me now,

in fractions, minutes, eons and degrees,
        like God's six working days,
so I can memorize them for *my* son,
        the stages I can name and praise

through fifteen billion years of space expanding
        like a pebble's ripples in a pool:
After the first tenth of a second passed,
        the universe commenced to cool;

        God saw that it was good,
and after just three minutes had gone by,
        less agitated then,
protons and neutrons merged as nuclei;

        and only after a brief
hundred thousand years, electrons could combine
        with nuclei—and thus
were atoms formed. "This universe of Mine

        is good, damned good, and some might say
My work's sensational," said God. And so it was
        that after a few billion years
our world began to look as presently it does—

        though when we're finished killing
off His whales, which no one living can recall,
        what story of us will be told
if He is there to tell it, after all?

PROTON DECAY

Most visible matter—stars, galaxies, and gas clouds—is made of hydrogen, and the nucleus of the hydrogen atom is a single proton. If protons decay, then the very substance of the universe is slowly rotting away like a cancer that infects matter itself. This rotting away of matter will, according to these unified [field] theories, take about a thousand billion billion (10^{21}) times the present age of the universe. We will have lots of time to explore the universe before it vanishes.

—HEINZ R. PAGELS, *The Cosmic Code*

From where I stand, Professor Pagels,
pausing in the tall grass as I climb the pathless hill
back to my house, picking wild asters for
the red vase on my window sill,

I say to you out loud *how much*—
how much I wish to dwell within the dwindling harvest
of my life a longer while,
how much our universe is blessed

simply by being here,
where nothing might have been, with still to go some
thousand billion billion times the age
we have already come

if matter is infected with such cancerous
but slow proton decay.
I greet your greeting to explore our universe
before time radiates away,

although, Professor, stranger, your
field theory estimate of crabbing time's disease
stretches the earthbound scale
of my mere mankind-measuring anxieties.

And yet I know that my wild asters
from the umbering, September valley hold
their glow for three days
in my house, their yellow centers tarnish into gold—

then they're forever gone,
partaking of disaster matter must at last
experience. Right now there are
more species than *this* griever in the parting grass

can keep at heart, in mind,
like Aromatic, Bushy, Calico, with purple blue,
and through the alphabet to Showy,
Upland White, and Willow, my thought-gifts to you,

my fellow mourner. So, let us
be bound by flowing grace
of words that cherish, words that touch across
what mortal time and space

remain, though even if we two could live to name
each single flower and each leaf,
those billions of last years before the end
would seem too sad, too brief,

when, inescapably, the end did come.
Always, in thought, the end nears now-death in our minds
outlives our life, it's part of us,
it's always what our wakeful searching finds,

and every flowered star we love
is brief as azure nightfall on this hill,
brief as companionable breath that lengthens into words
and then goes still.

NEANDERTHAL POEM, "AH," NUMBER ONE

Although one letter "a" is identical to another "a," words and sentences can be different. . . . Likewise, in our universe there are only a few fundamental building blocks: quarks, leptons, and gluons. These are the letters of the alphabet of nature. With this rather small alphabet, words are made—these are atoms. The words are strung together, with their own special grammar—the laws of quantum theory—to form sentences, which are molecules. Soon we have books, entire libraries, made out of molecular "sentences.". . . Out of identity came difference.

—Heinz R. Pagels, *The Cosmic Code*

Leaping leptons, gluons, and quarks—
difference from identity!
Sound me the *a*, Professor Pagels, from your name,
sound me a *b*;

ra! ra!, we've started, now a *c*,
ca-abracadabra—
dance me the prestidigitation of the alphabet
back to an *a* released as *ah!*

ah as in quark: and thus an *a*, conjoined
with *ah*, prolonged and rounded,
might have been the primal word
for joy unbounded

from astonished apelike lips—an *ah*, an *ahr*,
resounding from the lungs,
reverberating *hahr* up to the teeth,
until the tongue,

discovering a purpose to its taste,
plucked teasing, consonantal *t*,
and thus gave shape to *heart*,
atomic word for the anatomy

of art, for speech, *ah* yes, delighting
in its parts. Words are a lake
in which we look, Professor, partner, at
ourselves, reflecting what we make,

as morning brightens crimson in the mist,
from what we hear and see—
a rondo of frogs rumbling,
 light wind lilting lento in the willow tree.

Such mimic long *o* wind-words
bind us over silent distances, although
we two, in fact, have never met;
and yet in thought I go

with you where, glowing gluons, your thoughts go.
So if you read these
ahs, these *ohs,* this cry of origins,
call of identities,

perhaps you'll follow me over
the glade, over the clover-purple hill,
where once my father led me—
I can see him still—

to find the spring that starts the minnow stream
that sloshes pebbles burbling
through the pendant, orange jewelweed,
then bubbles loudly, merging

with the courting bullfrog bellows echoed
in the cattail marshes all
along the margins of the lake. There you can hear
the world's first bard Neanderthal

bleat out an *a* into an *ah!* And *oh,*
Professor Pagels, *ah* and *oo,*
across the separating spaces now,
from you to me and me to you,

molecular sentences flow
connecting differentiated strangers, *oo!* Trees
bloom with leaves of words; *ohs* blow
from the low lake to cool entire libraries.

THE INVISIBLE HAND

The best place to look for chaos is right in the atom. Although
individual random events [are] meaningless, the distribution of those
events . . . could be the subject of an exact science—probability
theory. . . . What is perceived as freedom by the individual is thus
necessity from a collective viewpoint. The die when it is thrown may
think it has freedom, but . . . it is part of a probability distribution;
it is being influenced by the invisible hand.

—HEINZ R. PAGELS, *The Cosmic Code*

I've never had much trouble finding chaos
even in the macroworld
of tables, chairs, and cats—especially
of kids! For sure, they're hurled

about by random energy, and all
a parent knows is: *move they must!*
Intention hardly matters, so hi-ho they're off—
bumped atoms in a cloud of dust.

When doing what their bodies
burn to do, thoughtless, they feel they're free,
while quantum theory says
dice-throwing probability,

fate's hand, determines with
a seven or a snake-eyes toss
the distribution of who wins and who craps out,
but not the consciousness of loss,

AUTUMN WARMTH

The universe today [with its background-radiation temperature measured to be 2.7 Kelvin] is the frozen remnant of the Big Bang. Like an ice crystal that has frozen out of a uniform water vapor, it has lots of structure—the galaxies, stars, and life itself. But according to the modern view, even the protons and neutrons—the very substance of matter—are the frozen fossils of the Big Bang. They too were created as temperature fell.

—HEINZ R. PAGELS, *Perfect Symmetry*

A fossil, yet I'm here, Professor Pagels,
      bare-armed in my garden, yanking out
      the wooden stakes supporting
my profuse tomato plants, now that the rout

      of robust weeds, twin triumph
with my bumper crop, has been concluded by
      the first October killing frost
         last night's unclouded sky

made unpreventable. Low morning sun
         softens the nestling air,
and, slowly, I absorb its bleak, mild rays.
      Hornets bore in the rotting pears

         clinging from loosened stems;
      wasps in the spider-threaded eaves
         deliriously thrum,
as if their armored bodies must believe

         their harvest will not end. Shaken,
scraped clean, for next year's use, of clotted soil,
      the stakes go bundled to the shed;
the Rototiller, drained of gas and oil,

hunches beside the hanging row
of shovels, hoes, and rakes, dreaming of upturned stones;
                a sluggish garter snake
slips past a silhouette of crushed toad bones.

        Along the stacked, dry boulder wall
that frames the sweep of my whole lawn, borders
            my garden, and asserts my place,
I pile leftover green tomatoes, pumpkins, gourds—

        my galaxy of vegetables—
as testimony that I lived here, too,
                with all my fellow fossils—
            protons, neutrons, yes, and you,

Professor, whom I picture with a huge
                thermometer, rectal,
of course (just like the one my mother used),
                still measuring the spectral

background radiation of the universe—
                a frozen remnant of
Big Bang whose one fireball creative secret,
            like a god's initiating love

embodied, merely was to let things cool.
            Now I can see along the margin
of the steady lake, the spreading aggregate
                of simple grains, the faint, thin

glaze of ice; and now, condensed, night's vapor
                on a shaded willow tree,
leaf after leaf, reveals its crystal hexagons—
            hint of the perfect symmetry

before the cosmic cooling started. Yet
            I know that too much cold
can uncreate created living form.
        Our season in the sun grows old,

        although there is enough
      warmth left at least to keep me awed
at my awareness of myself as remnant,
        gourd or green tomato, flawed

so lately into life—according to the clock
       of temperature decrease. As one
fossil to another, "Please put down your thermometer
         and join me in the sun!"

NEUTRINOS

In spite of their enormous numbers, [neutrinos] do not contribute much to the total mass of the universe. But if they have mass, then it is estimated that they would account for ninety percent of all the mass of the universe—an invisible mass, because no one can actually see this neutrino "background radiation." The other 10 percent—the minor part—is the visible matter in the form of stars and galaxies. Neutrinos could thus account for the "missing mass"—the amount required to halt the expansion of the universe and cause it, finally, to contract.

—HEINZ PAGELS, *The Cosmic Code*

This fall I'm rooting for contraction!
Please, Professor Pagels, find the missing mass
that would assure mankind
expansion will reverse and bring to pass

the ultimate collapse,
some distant but inevitable day,
of matter on itself. I'd know
the universe would go its wished-for way

returning to the nothing
it originated from; Big Bang would detonate
space-time into existence
once again, and once again our fate

would be a universe of gas
expanding into stars and galaxies.
Such cycles breathing out
and breathing in—eternities

unto themselves—depend upon the gravity
of background radiation. Oh!
my happy, holiest of rounded hopes
is that invisible neutrinos
possess the needed mass

to keep the universe from thinning out forever
        to a lifeless void, a bland,
undifferentiated cosmic mist, never

        to be born again, never to fashion
suns and moons, rivers, forests, mountains, trees,
        a planet tilted on its axis
for each seasons' sake (at twenty-three degrees),

        migrating robins, crocuses,
            red tulips, daffodils,
then summer lilies, honeysuckle, columbine,
        (how eagerly each sweet name trills

liltingly on the tongue to welcome them!)
        and on to autumn when
the valley fills with aster, hyssop, goldenrod,
        until first snow skips back again

and pale narcissus, sprouting inside by a window
        in a blue, ceramic bowl,
unfold the bloom of their aroma in the dawn.
        To love the universe, the whole

flowering pageant of emerging forms, always
        has meant we've hoped for the return
of each leaf, permanent in paradise, and yet
        I know that we must learn

recurrence can't restore what's *here*: moonlight
        bestowing stillness on my wife,
my sunlit daughter savoring a peach,
        my own remaining life.

Professor, if your blank neutrino does
        have any mass at all,
a tilted planet would fulfill my mortal wish
        for springtime, summer, winter, fall.

THE RED SHIFT

The discovery of the expansion of the universe [was made) by Edwin Hubble in 1929–1931. He observed that the red shift of the light from distant galaxies is proportional to their distance from us. His conclusion is based on the fact that an atom which is moving away from us at high velocity, such as in a distant galaxy, has its spectral lines shifted to the red in proportion to its velocity.

—Heinz R. Pagels, *The Cosmic Code*

I'll bet that Hubble made
his mind-bending discovery
by first observing in
himself a red shift in the galaxy

of his own past, watching the boy
who he once was recede
knee-deep across the waving grass
at hazy dawn where windblown roses breed

in scrubby patches by the cliff.
He sees him carrying a bright red pail
to put collected seashells in
as he descends, holding the driftwood rail

his father made from ribs of boats,
down to the dunes that curve
along the bay and arc the eye
out to a spit of shore, then, with a swerve,

still farther out, beyond
the current, churning water green to blue,
where a red buoy gongs its bell
and resonates. Oh, I can hear it, too,

Professor Pagels, look;
returning on the beach, that's me
precisely as I was,
poking a tentacled anemone,

while swift bank swallows whir
and swoop into their nesting holes
in colonies along the sandy cliffs,
and gulls dive in the shoals

squawking for broken crabs crushed in the tide.
The past is *now* wherever light
arrives in shifts of red
from galaxies whose distant flight

must be proportional
to the velocity at which they move away.
I see the boy's red pail;
I hear the buoy bell—as if that day

came back . . . but not to be possessed.
It comes back as the loss
of what it was—absence made palpable—
with all the glinting dross

of scallop shells and mandibles and claws
filling the foaming rush
of slushing tide along the shore—
without the grainy touch,

the suck of feet upon wet sand.
And now, in my own shifting sight, I feel
increasing distance from
my recollecting self, who seems unreal

to me—a me that's even
separated from the cliff here where I stand,
my present life. Moving away
from that boy, swinging his bright, shell-filled pail,

who hears a buoy bell
that long ago has ceased to ring,
moving away from the observer that I am
this misted, swirling dawn, singing

a red song to myself
among the flowing, windblown grass, I see
my life arrive light years from now,
complete, at someone else's galaxy.

OUT OF NOTHING

The answer to the question "Where did the universe come from?" is
that it came out of the vacuum. The entire universe is a reexpression of
sheer nothingness. . . . If you add up all the energy in the universe it
almost adds up to zero. [On the negative side] there is the potential
of the gravitational attraction of the various galaxies for each
other. . . . On the positive side of the ledger is the mass energy of all the
particles in the universe. . . . If the two numbers matched, the total
energy of the universe would be zero, and it wouldn't take any energy to
create the universe.

—HEINZ R. PAGELS, *The Cosmic Code*

That's good to hear, Professor
Pagels, now
that I feel so fatigued,
so emptied out by husbanding
and fathering, beleaguered

by the pleading needs of family
and friends
I need to care about, although
it takes more summoned will
each day not to let caring go

back to the vacuum
out of which it came, that equipoise
of numbers matched at zero
energy—
silent, without the noise

of hissing cosmic dust, vibrating stars
that groan in drumroll thunderclaps.
My peace, eased free of consciousness, would be
old zero's gift, and yet, perhaps

aware of universal nothingness, my self
might still exist somehow
by knowing that no self is there.
Since multiplying zero does allow

a vacuum to create,
perhaps my own unbodied mind might be
the lilting, melancholy movement
of a Mozart symphony

expounding on a minor chord
until blank nothingness becomes a flute run
balanced by a violin's reply.
Selfless at last—un-

burdened back to careless rest, back to the void
of undivided night,
the symmetry before, *ex nihilo*, the Big Bang,
like Jehovah's cry, "Let there be light!"

began the prayer of mind
in lamentation to return to dust,
to particles, to primal
zero, our first home—would I then know the thrust

of nothing to express itself,
creating matter and creating space,
as if I were a messenger
of cosmic absence, yes, as if my human face

were destined to appear,
and after me, my children, too—
with space inventing time?
But now, Professor Pagels, brother, you,

compounded double of myself,
appear reposing in exhaustion of your own
with bare November nearing
as, reflected blazing on a lakefront stone

your unborn son will step upon,
sweetness of evening light leaps up, and, yes,
you feel the surging countersweet
of sheerest emptiness.

THE BLACK HOLE

Imagine [that] the whole mass of the sun is crushed down to a radius
of a few kilometers. The gravity and space curvature near this
compacted sun is enormous. If a light beam were sent out to hit and
bounce off this object, it would never return .... Since light cannot leave
this object, it "appears" as a black hole in space .... An observer who fell
into the center of a black hole could see time slow down. But the falling
observer can never communicate his strange experience to his friend
outside.

—Heinz R. Pagels, *Perfect Symmetry*

My brother and I planned to meet
at our secluded campsite up in Maine
beside an azure lake
swarming with rainbow trout. I'd hired a local plane

to fly me to our dock, but when
I saw how beaten up it was, how queerly
the old pilot squinted upwind
at the sun, I felt a fleeting shock of fear.

A reject of the Wright Brothers?
Or had he built it with his son—sort of
a modern Daedalus?
Its banged pontoons were dented right above

the water line which seemed to me
too high for the sad bird to lift its ass
for takeoff. But, by God,
it did! The pilot made, I thought, a needless pass

between two quarry walls,
then brushed the treetops just to show
where a tornado scythed
a highway through the woods, ten years ago,

which wound back on itself.
When we arrived, my waiting brother waved his hands
wildly from the dock's edge.
The pilot asked, "How's 'bout before we land

we do a couple lucky loops?"
The first loop made me squeeze
my thighs against my groin, and with the second,
wider loop, the engine wheezed,

shuddered and stopped. We slid into a nosedive,
spinning toward the evening sun
reflected in the lake. Oh, I was falling
through my mind's black hole, the one

curved space to float me home,
so slowly I had time to think that I
alone had nothing left to know
except the circle of the sun within the sky

inside the water, blue advancing
bluer into brighter blue—
although my unbelieving brother held his hands
over his face. And you,

Professor Pagels, would you not have seen,
reflected in my eyes,
the unresisted pull into the perfect heart
of orange light, the last surprise

of pure acceptance that can never pass
beyond itself? I guess
the gas ran back into the engine,
for we leveled out, and, yes,

terror returned the instant we touched down,
and my taut body knew
that I was safe there in my brother's arms.
Next morning my whole chest was bruised

where I had clutched myself, and one week later,
back in the old river town
by the abandoned mill, we learned my pilot's plane
had crashed in the dense mountain

flying home. "Don't know how Joel lasted
long's he did," his neighbor said.
We sat, a covenant of brothers by the fire,
and yet the orange-red,

the green-blue flames distracted me; I watched
the sizzling rainbow trout that night,
its smeared red stripe surrounded by black dots—
collapsed suns lost in their trapped light.

NUMBER

The nothingness "before" the creation of the universe is the most complete
void that we can imagine—no space, time, or matter existed. It is a world
without place, without duration or eternity, without number . . . Yet
this unthinkable void converts itself into the plenum of existence—into
necessary consequence of physical laws. Where are these laws written into
the void? What "tells" the void that it is pregnant with a possible universe?

—HEINZ R. PAGELS, *Perfect Symmetry*

Mothering void, ripe emptiness,
pregnant with number—*one,*
the number first of all for the duration
each of us enjoys beneath the sun,

our single sun, and yet a minor star among
such billions in the Milky Way,
I thank you for one lifetime
being what I am before the day

I separate into more stable particles.
Thanks, equally, for *two,*
the other by which one conceives oneself as one,
apart, and yet a part of you,

O void unthinkable, your child of place—
this cooling quantum mess
of hydrogen and helium, of chairs and cats,
your unknown law of nothingness

converted to the plenum of existence like
the animals from Noah's ark
who clump the ramp boards, bumping on their way
where light breaks through the fertile dark.

We two together now in thought,
Professor Pagels, let's give thanks to *three*—
perhaps three apples in a bowl,
or, in a cherry tree,

three calling birds whose random voices
blend within the mind
and on their branches make a triangle
should I elect to find

a pattern there. To meet my need,
another bird alights,
an oriole, and lo!, a rectangle appears,
as through the summer nights

the constellation, Leo Minor, guards
my dreaming house, accompanied
by five-starred Lyra's harp chords in the wind
while multiplying numbers breed

their imaged offspring in the womb of sleep.
So I recite myself among
the stars, the crystal hexagons of snow,
electrons, protons—each one sung

for its own numbered self to celebrate
possible matter, time, and space,
including me to think of the unthinkable,
to give the pregnant void a face

(only a while, a nanosecond measured
even by our finite sun)
yet long enough to call her *Mother*, long enough to count
from zero up to number one.

OUTLASTING YOU

Heinz R. Pagels, an experienced climber, fell to his death from a peak
in Colorado on July 24,1988, at the age of 49. He had written: "I
dreamt I was clutching at the face of a rock but it would not hold.
Gravel gave way. 1 grasped for a shrub, but it pulled loose, and in cold
terror I fell into the abyss. But I realized that what I embody, the principle
of life, cannot be destroyed. It is written into the cosmic code, the
order of the universe. As I continued to fall in the dark void, embraced
by the vault of the heavens, I sang to the beauty of the stars and made
my peace with the darkness."

And now, unfathomably soon,
dear Heinz, a first *good-bye;* I had not dreamed
I would endure outlasting you.
I wonder if it seemed,

in that suspended interval,
though still obedient
to cosmic laws, you had outlived
your final fears because somehow you meant

to choose your accident amid
such stony randomness
and thus keep true a wide-eyed vow to live
in touch with your abyss—

darkness encoded in the vault
of your reflecting mind.
Dwelling on your own corresponding stars,
you had rehearsed your death to find

the right last thought that might
contain eternity: the gravel giving way,
the grasping for a prickly shrub—
its snug roots, pallid gray,

suddenly naked in the sun.
And then, before acceleration starts,
as if the air will hold
your body up, there's time to feel your heart

push forth a surge of blood;
there's time to feel a gasp leap out,
expanding from your lungs,
a cringing whisper first, and then a shout,

embodied as a scream.
A *NO,* a full, involuntary *NO,*
unwinds as if from someone else,
another life below,

preceding yours, your father's cry,
a stranger's, or perhaps
you hear my decomposing voice
come echoing unloosed from a crevasse.

Descending with my arms outstretched—
my knees like twin moons orbiting my head—
through my own galaxy,
a shrub uprooted from its gravel bed

like a commanding scepter
in my hand, I try deliberately now
to dream your liberating dream
of the encompassing abyss, of how,

at last, you sang out to the stars.
Though soon, my friend, it will not matter who
preceded whom, tonight
at home I cannot follow you

unfathomably light
in thought embracing the indifferent air.
With my grief's *NO* upon my lips,
appalled because you summoned me to dare

to make peace with the dark that lasts
so everlasting long,
I'm earthbound with *good-bye,* but bless you for
the starlit beauty of your song.

FROM
Inheritance
(1999)

((

THE CAVE OF LASCAUX

One frieze shows a buffalo disemboweled by a spear through its
hindquarters; a stick-figure man whose head is that of a bird and who is
falling backward in front of the buffalo; a pole with a bird on it below
the man; and to the left, behind the man, a two-horned rhinoceros.

—John E. Pfeiffer, *The Emergence of Man*

Among the shaded animals,
the potent bison, the rhinoceros,
rendered with rounded grace,
a figure of a man killed in a hunt,
stick-thin, a birdlike face,

appears as if scrawled by a child.
Why should the human form
be drawn as if it were a toy
to be discarded at a whim? Perhaps
the artist found no joy

in contemplation of himself, compared
with what he witnessed in the world
of claw and fang, of skull and skeleton,
astounding in variety
beyond what anyone

could find by looking inward. Ohl
behind his eyes a darkness must have swirled
in which fear lacked the shape
to be revealed, until
the high curve of the bison's bristled nape,

repeated in the bowed head,
the eviscerated belly, could release that fear
by making it hold still
for contemplation on the stone,
thus to be seen at will

as beautiful. What had begun in fear,
the hunt's necessity, was changed
when recreated by
himself. Those represented animals
stepped forth beneath his inner sky

of dawning thought, immersed in his own light.
And so he took dominion as
his inner world and outer merged into
a vast continuum
of fear and beauty from whose depths a new,

abstracted sense of hope emerged.
If he could picture animals so clearly when
their bodies were not there,
keep them from vanishing, would not
he, too, return somewhere

when someone in the sky who shaped the clouds
depicted him? And once he could
revive the bison he had killed,
kneeling to meet their image in a pool,
then every absence might be filled

with what was lost. Descended from him now
to disillusioned emptiness,
I conjure him inside
his fire-lit cave, crouched and contemplative,
enraptured as his deft hands slide

across the shimmered surface of the wall
where bison browse across the fields,
each circle of their eyes edged still in place
with stony permanence,
his bird-head changed into a human face.

THE DEAD KING

The dead king of Eynan was propped on a pillow of stones in about 9,000 B.C. . . . . The red-painted parapet and its top tier of a hearth [at the burial site] were a response to the decomposition of his body. For a long time, the smoke from its holy fire was a source of hallucinations and commands that controlled the Mesolithic world of Eynan.

—JULIAN JAYNES, *The Origin of Consciousness*

Without your laws directing us,
we don't know whom it's right to execute;
we don't know whom to spare.
We've propped your head upon the stones,
laid out your crown and staff, and taken care

to paint the parapet
in royal red, according to your wish,
that even in your sleep
you'll still remember and you'll speak to us.
We've built a hearth on top to keep

the holy fire always burning there,
and in the smoke at dawn
we see your spirit beckoning
for us to grope and pray,
to sacrifice whatever flesh can bring

pungent aroma to your senses
so you savor it upon the air.
And if our worship pleases you,
and if you would protect us
as in life, tell us, your children, what to do—

tell us if we should carve
a figure out of wood or clay
to keep you steady in our memory—
cupped ears, an open mouth,
round staring eyes that let you see

we are still listening,
we never will forget. Nothing has changed
despite the absence of your lips
upon our lips, despite
the stillness of your bones and the eclipse

of sunlight by the moon
that left vast darkness with us on the day
you made your final choice
to seek your ancestors. Your oldest son
confessed that he can't hear your voice.

We think he should be banished;
maybe death should be his punishment
for blasphemy. But we don't know!
We can't decide how to decide. And now I hear
your grave command that I must go

out to the wilderness
to fast and clear the rival voices
speaking in my head. Then I'll be sure
some spirit that our brother
has offended, who cannot endure

the spirit of his life, has not
turned me against him by assuming your voice
at the altar of my mind.
The dark smoke gestures me away;
perhaps I'll never find

sweet certainty again. I have displeased you.
Now the windy smoke
of your great anger grinds my eyes,
commanding me to etch this in the stone,
commanding me to exorcise

whatever voices still resist your voice,
contending that your voice alone—
one voice and one decree—
rules in the heavens and on earth, that only
in obedience can I be free.

GRANDEUR

Thus, from the war of nature, from famine and death, the most exalted object which we are capable of conceiving, namely, the production of the higher animals, directly follows. There is grandeur in this view of life . . . whilst this planet has gone cycling according to the fixed law of gravity, from so simple a beginning endless forms most beautiful and most wonderful have been, and are being evolved.

—CHARLES DARWIN, *The Origin of Species*

You've made it clear, Charles Darwin, why
famine and war and failure
are inevitable—thus our highest cause
must be to contemplate
the twisting rabbit in the fox's jaws

as evolution's art,
as if our species' brains had been designed
for awe: to witness a parade
of stalking creatures softly passing through.
Contrived to be unmade

by the same law, as fixed as gravity,
that made them from a single cell
in what, we can surmise,
had been the simplest of beginnings, they
have learned to use their eyes

to find their prey, avoid detection—anything
to keep themselves alive
another second in the sun—
while we, on high above the higher animals,
are free to stand apart for one

stunned blink of cosmic time
in which we flourish, to observe our fate.
I watch my life unfold
as if it were the story of a distant friend;
although he has grown old,

his daily correspondence keeps me young
as his observer, permanent
in speculation. No,
I am not fooled; I don't believe him
when he says, while pausing in the swirling snow

as he is splitting wood,
or standing in his garden with an eggplant
like a planet in his palm,
that fifteen million years of human life can be
held still in a containing calm;

not so, the letters tremble
where he signs his name, and I can hear
his moaning smothered in his sleep.
And yet his sorrow still seems beautiful
from the calm distance that I keep—

the distance thought allows,
the highest view that you can take
in seeing grandeur as new forms replace
their predecessors with no end
in sight. Your wonder helps me see my face

in both the rabbit and the fox,
and when I feel
exalted,
I conceive a species someday will evolve
whose sense of grandeur is
so absolute that they will solve

the ultimate enigma of regret—
grieving for loss that life
can't thrive without—by celebrating everything
merely for being what it is:
both here and vanishing—

forever gone, forever having been,
forever unrepeatable.
And now the lumbering brontosaur browses past,
and now the mastodon,
and now, Charles Darwin, you at last—

yourself a radical mutation, so
extreme that human thought
never shall be the same again.
And now my turn is come
to watch my friend fade out, as when

one wave, rampaging in,
merges with backflow surging from the shore;
or when the dissipating dew
dissolves into a mist, and with low, morning wind
the white mist filters through

the valley, pausing in the marsh
among stiff cattails and bright jewelweed,
then ambles on—although
some rebel grandeur in my heart resists
my willingness to let him go.

WATCHERS

Photographed from the moon, [the Earth] seems to be a kind of organ-
ism. It's plainly in the process of developing, like an enormous embryo.
It is, for all its stupendous size and the numberless units of its life
forms, coherent. Every tissue is linked for its viability to every other
tissue.

—LEWIS THOMAS, *The Medusa and the Snail*

And so I'm linked to you
like cells within a growing embryo,
and you are linked to me,
and we, together, linked to everyone
as watchers from the moon can see.

The patient watchers from the moon can tell
what currents pushing through the tide
direct vast spawning from the swaying deep,
and what ancestral pathways
through the buoyant air wedged wild geese keep

inscribed within their brains
that safely store stupendous images—
range after range of mountain snow,
and shadowed woodland green,
blue sky reflected in blue sea below.

Although they see all parts as one,
Wholly dependent and yet numberless,
the watchers from the moon
surmise some flaw may be developing,
some rampant cells may soon

outgrow the rest, presuming that their lives
were all life meant. And yet
for now, the watchers still are full
of admiration, awe;
each tissue seems connected, viable—

like you and me, together,
linked as one with our increasing kind,
taking dominion everywhere,
now cultivating forests, now the seas,
now blasting even through the air.

The membrane of the sky
holds in accumulated oxygen,
welcomes the visible, good light,
protects from lethal ultraviolet,
and guards against the flight

of random meteors that burn out,
harmless at the edge of our home space, as if
by miracle, although
just friction from our atmosphere is what
the watchers from the moon must know

keeps us alive and linked
each to the other, each to the sunlit cycles
of exhaling plants and trees.
For pollination, fruits and flowers have
warm winds and their obliging bees;

forests renew themselves from their decay,
aided by intermittent rain;
and plankton, drifting in the sun to breed,
provide the herring and the whale
with all the food they need

to keep revolving life alive
in this appointed place—
to which we're linked and which replenishes
ambrosia of the air
and animates the sea that says:

Coherence is the law
we must obey, although the watchers see
certain relentless cells below,
dividing, and divided from the rest,
forming a monster embryo.

BOUNTY

Incredible elaborations of the flowering plants kept exploding. The
angiosperms had taken over the world. Grass was beginning to cover
the bare earth, and all kinds of vines and bushes squirmed and writhed
under new trees with flying seeds. . . . Apes [evolved into] men because
flowers had produced seeds and fruits in such tremendous quantities
that a new and totally different store of energy had become available.

—LOREN EISLEY, *The Immense Journey*

Here come exploding waves
of wind-borne ovaries with seeds inside,
each like a little astronaut—
angiosperms are landing everywhere,
they've taken hold, having been taught
by parent genes to hunker down, dig in,
grasp hard, and cling with fibrous roots.
Incredible elaborations now appear
by rivers and by lakes,
in forests, deserts, plains—they settle here

with power to proliferate,
creeping or swaying, climbing, reaching out;
each in its own determined way
appropriates a space
in which to greet the light, where it can stay.

The mustard family,
the family of peas, of carrot, and of mint,
the aster-daisy family,
stretch out as squirming vine or writhing bush;
extending even to the sea,

they cover every barren inch of earth.
The grasses, ah, the grasses,
thousands of rough, colonizing variants
are replicating what they are—
as if the only sense

under the photosynthesizing sun
is to renew yourself
a millionfold into a universe of seeds
that flowers always into *you,*
a universe that breeds,

yes, *you,* again and yet again
with no end but your own prodigious self,
unchanged, becoming more,
still more, of what precisely you have been.
But now a totally new store

of vital energy,
a grazer's plenitude, transforms how eating
fares upon the fertile earth.
Plants must make way for ungulates, and thus
devourers flourish at the birth

of still another era
as the world becomes a cornucopia—
a romping goat god's gift to please
the dazed apes gaping at
such quantities of fruit upon the trees

it seems provided just for them.
For them the bushes flower
and the shrubs, the vines, the pungent herbs;
for them red berries ripen as exploding
bounty of the earth disturbs

their sweetened lips to shape
their needed words, "All mine, all this is mine!"
until an echo from the sky
rolls out as a resounding, absolute command:
Be fruitful, multiply,

replenish all the earth, subdue the beasts,
and take dominion over
every living thing! becomes their holy text,
though some hunched fear within their seed
dreads what dominion will seize power next.

FORGETTING TO FORGET

The mark of the new evolution which sweeps us along is that unlearning and learning anew have already become as important to survival as learning used to be. . . . The question for the future is whether we can be taught to forget as effectively as we remember.

—JOHN E. PFEIFFER, *The Emergence of Man*

Perhaps I'll get good at forgetting what
    no longer is of use to know,
unless, my dear, through inattention I forget
    the new rules of survival say
        I can't be finished yet

    unlearning what I learned if I
am thinking I must still expunge from thought
    thoughts that had once distracted me-
like the uneven upturn of your lip.
        Suggesting that I see

a shifting smile and a seductive frown
    appear together, you reveal
how meaning still refuses to hold still.
        What use at this late hour
    are random memories that fill

my mind with more distractions, so I'll add
    your wistful smile-frown to my list
of images I must remember to let go,
        and then I'll have to add
your gaudy, patchwork hat—there's no

    utility in keeping
    such a silly hat in mind;
you bought it on a whim as to say:
    it's autumn everywhere I
my brazen colors never fade away.

And on one Halloween,
I placed it jauntily askew upon
    a grinning pumpkin head
  so that the trick-or-treating kids,
placated by bright orange and bold red

    and a blue bowl of Milky Ways,
would leave our house to slower ravages
    of parching and fiddling sleet.
    I'll mark your hat down for
my next oblivion, and I'll repeat

    the words that clue me in
to what I must remember to forget:
    a pumpkin's frost-defying face,
your tilted smile-frown, and our rain-streaked house.
    But now from some unbidden place,

from nowhere I can clearly recognize,
    music comes throbbing in
like evening light, and for the life of me
    I can't connect it to its source.
It could be anybody's memory—

    a dream of water flowing or
of wind unfurling in snow-laden pines,
    so how can I unlearn it, though
    I need to move ahead,
stripped-down and free? I need to go

with the new strategy of survival
    that's sweeping me along,
unburdened with mementos from the past,
    and I'm reminded once again
I must forget your hat; it too at last

must be obliterated like
the crowning crescent of the clouded moon,
        although I still can hear
        collective music streaming in
from somewhere both so distant and so near

        that I can't stop the surge
of images such music summons from
        the upswell of my mind.
        And now I see my mother's hat,
its flaring, rounded brim, and now I find

        I'm picturing the feathers I
            once stole from its brown band.
Her knitted hat stretched tightly on her head,
            her fuzzy earmuffs on,
grandmother pulls me on my sled

as my white dog leaps at me from behind,
        yanks off my pomponed hat
        and trots away, snout high, uphill
            beyond the frozen stream.
Way up there on the ridge I see him still

        in perfect silhouette,
        my limp hat flapping from his mouth,
and after him another prancing canine friend—
        then yet another in a line
            that seems to have no end

    and leads somewhere beyond sight.
        I can't say where they went,
my dear, each dangling someone's hat, and yet
        they're prancing to the music still
that I keep on forgetting to forget.

THE DWARF AND DOCTOR FREUD

Freud bled heavily both during and after the procedure [to remove a lesion from his palate] and was made to lie down on a cot "in a tiny room in a ward of the hospital." His only companion was another patient, whom Anna Freud described later as a "nice, friendly," retarded dwarf. . . . [Freud] had rung the bell for help, but the bell was out of order. Unable to make himself heard, Freud was helpless. Fortunately, the dwarf rushed out to get the nurse.

—PETER GAY, *Freud: A Life for Our Time*

I don't know why they had to put him
in the same room they put me.
He didn't drop his eyes as usually they do;
he looked at me—he couldn't speak—
to say, *I'm here because I'm bleeding too.*

He must have been important
since they kept repeating, "Doctor Freud;'
when making him lie down
and telling him to rest. I was afraid.
I thought that he would drown

in all the blood that blistered
from the bandages around his nose. And yet
something about the way
he searched my face put me at ease,
as if we'd met before or if he knew one day

he'd find a cure. But that's a dream.
No one can cure what I have wrong with me.
I have to take me as I am and go
with how things are. And maybe that is true
for everyone, although

I had to do something right then
about the doctor's overflowing blood.
I think that he could tell
he was in danger just by looking
at my face. He tried to ring the bell,

but it was broken, and help
didn't come. He stared at it
as though a glare from him might make it work;
he rang it harder, gave up, lay back
coughing with a jerk

that shook his eyes, and then I realized
I'd have to help, although
I'm not a doctor, and I knew
I never could explain
why God makes dwarfs or puts some people through

such useless suffering and shame
for which there is no cure.
They told me to lie still on my own cot, but he
was bleeding. He could not cry out
or get the bell to ring, and I could see

a kind of quiet in his eyes
that comes from looking inside at yourself—
as I do sometimes late at night—
and I decided not
to stay still as they said, that I was right

to leave the room and get the nurse,
although she yelled at me
and wouldn't listen; she kept pushing me away.
"He'll choke!" I shouted—then
she followed as I led to where he lay,

his white hands folded on his chest,
his face, too, white like moonlight
on the marshes of the Zuyder Zee
where I fished with my father as a boy,
not knowing I was free

to love him till he drowned. Doctor Freud's daughter
thanked me later as they left
and asked my name, but then a howling flood
of distant faces filled my mind.
        I can't explain it, but I answered, "Blood."

THE BEAR ON THE UNICYCLE

The fact that in certain circumstances bears ride unicycles and dolphins
never do is not evidence that unicycle riding was adaptive among bear
ancestors and unadaptive among dolphin ancestors, nor is it evidence
that bears in a natural habitat necessarily do anything that is analogous
to unicycle riding.

—DONALD SYMONDS, *The Evolution of Human Sexuality*

I wonder whether writing poems,
like trained bears riding unicycles, falls
within the category of
unfit behavior, nonadaptive, thus not linked
to our survival, but to love

for doing something for its own skewed sake,
simply for fun, whose meaning lies
precisely in its blithe irrelevance.
Cycling around a circle and
refusing to make sense

(since it does not make sense to live
by sense alone) is tantamount to saying that
here's what I do: I'm fit to dance—
take heed, adaptive listeners—that gives me
no advantage in the chance

my genes have to reduplicate themselves,
yet makes my routine bearable.
So picture me tricked out in a red cap,
a tight red jacket with
brass buttons on the cuffs, and on my lap

an oversized harmonica
to play my swirling circus music while
I ride nowhere upon my wheel,
keeping my balance as I go around
by feeling what I feel

needs no objective other than
the need to keep on feeling what I feel,
as long as I can play
(spokesman of sorts) my notable harmonica
the nonadaptive way

my wish for immortality turns back
upon myself. Bear with me now
in this my finest fit; I swear I'll get around
to what I have to say—
yes, even in this poem, though it may sound

too circular for you to get
a handle on my meaning in the way
I mean my whirling words,
my nonadaptive nonsense, to make sense.
Unlike migrating birds

or fish that swim upstream to spawn,
who have a purpose going where they go;
unlike our ancestor
who first contrived a wheel to get somewhere,
not merely make a metaphor

for fortune's fickleness,
I choose to find direction by
remaining where I am, though not remaining still,
as if my habitat of words
were nature made anew, as if my human will

could hold us in a circle where
you can approve my bearing my own soul
boldly in the fit cause
of improvising limpid laughter—laughter
breeding her own laws.

Since my own barely noticeable life
can't come around again,
I tip my cap to all those wheeling stars above—
my nonsense fare-thee-well which is
not linked to my survival, but to love.

THE LONG AND THE SHORT OF WHAT'S GOOD
AND WHAT'S BAD

In all languages studied to date the word good appears more often than
the word for bad. (In English, good appears five times more often than
its opposite.) But what are we to make of the fact that long occurs far
more frequently than short?

—John E. Pfeiffer, *The Emergence of Man*

In every language studied up to now,
the word for good appears
outbalancing the word for bad.
It seems our wishful species would deny
a darker truth. I think that's sad,

for in the long run we can't beat death's rap;
it can't be good to fool ourselves.
How bad can bad death be—what we most dread—
if shortly we will not
be conscious of our being dead?

Death is just—normal. Only a bad god
would have the gall to plan
that long-unwary matter should eventually
grow conscious of its dying self,
as if the whirling universe we see

evolved into a looking glass.
Thought is an accident,
a bad mutation in the drift of things
that can't be counted on to serve
survival long, although, in short, thought brings

good feelings to a higher pitch.
It's good to sing out, "O, I'm feeling good!"
when watching how the dawn
paints berries on the dogwood tree,
makes me Mozartian, makes me feel drawn

out of myself, *ecstatic,*
as the rooted meaning of that word connotes.
Yet also, by its nature, thought
reminds us we must say good-bye to everything
love touches on; we're caught

in picturing the windy snow
as summer sunlight settles in the corn.
Just as good-morning words
leap forth melodic from our lips,
then what we named, white blossoms and red birds,

are stopped short in the past. That's bad.
It's bad to see our lives fade in the mist;
it's bad when downbeat thoughts create
a laughless self that can't
detach itself from its own body's fate.

I'm a short person, though I write
long poems. I played shortstop at school and made
the long throw from the grass with ease;
I'm still short-tempered, yet my friends have stayed tuned
long enough to please

my aching sense that of all goods
friendship is best. And yet
I won't allow myself one song
surmising my life lives one short leap past
my burial; I do not long

for terminal eternity. I think
it's good to face what's bad;
that's what a poem must do or else it lies.
Let me remind you, loyal pal,
my body knows what "short-of-breath" implies;

the long scar down my chest
attests to that. Here's what I want:
as purple evening pauses
in my dogwood tree, I want to even out the odds
that favor bad hope since hope causes

us to lie—as if good-byes really were good;
they're not. We can't kill death
even in thought, and thought cannot be killed
the short time we're alive. Listen,
my long-enduring friend, for I'm now filled

with noteworthy resolve
to balance nature's thoughtless balances
of good—short life with bad—long death
with balance of my own,
my weighted words of measured breath.

For my finale I need one last short
refrain for good and bad,
and even if my scorekeeping is wrong,
I've still made good composing offbeat
Balance you can count on—if you laugh along.

Fathering The Map
(1993)

❨

WILD TURKEYS IN PARADISE

Just down the slope from my own deck,
two apple trees I planted years ago,
now fully grown, stretch out their arms
as if they are enjoying the late warmth
of the November sun.
They bore so many apples that
I let them ripen unplucked on the branch
and fall, according to the rhythm of the year.
Such bounty piled up on the ground
the grazing deer could not
consume them as they rotted and turned brown,
and I could smell their pungency
when wind blew from the east
until the first snow came and covered them.
Last Sunday, strutting stupid from the woods—as if
no hunters stalked Vermont—
six turkeys gathered by the trees,
bobbing their jowly heads beneath the snow
to slurp the apple nectar, so fermented that
just twenty minutes later
they were reeling, and their eyes
blazed with amazing knowledge that transported them,
within their bodies, into paradise.
Despite their drunkenness,
despite the ice that kept them shifting one foot
to the frozen next,
they kept their balance in a dance
of bumping lightly up against each other,
circling, brushing wings, and then—
as if their inner music paused—
they'd dip their heads back underneath the snow
and lift them up so high
their necks stretched out to twice their length
to let the trickling juice prolong their ecstasy.
And thus unfolds a moral tale:

To be plain stupid is
to be divinely blessed, and lacking that
transcendent gift, an animal advanced as I
requires a holiday
to cultivate stupidity, to choose
one Sunday morning to know
nothing of ongoing hunger but
my body trembling in the sun,
drunk on itself, so that right here on earth,
right now, I tasted paradise—
as, so to speak, in talking turkey, I now do.
My pilgrim mind has taken flight
and then returned to join
my body stomping in the snow; and so
I raise a toast to say:
I give thanks in behalf of six dazed, drunken birds
that grace the icy view
beneath my apple trees today!

STELLAR THANKSGIVING

Thanks to the huger stars
whose furnaces burned hot enough
in million sizzling billions of degrees
to cook up heavy elements from nuclei
of hydrogen and helium
like carbon, iron, silicon, for without these
proliferating life
never could have emerged:
no algae snoozing blissful in their slime,
no plants to fill the atmosphere
with oxygen for later forms in their good time
to welcome to their lungs,
no leaning grasses on the dunes,
and on the shore no shells, no spiny ruins
to testify who vanished there,
no flowers for the pollinating bees,
no hymning trees to strum the air,
no lidless reptiles blinking in the sun,
no flashing multitudes of fish,
no congregated birds, not one;
no mice, no moles, no mammals, monkeys,
not Australopithecus,
Neanderthal, Cro-Magnon, us,
who are the means,
as if determined from the start,
by which stars comprehend
their evolutionary roles,
how some turn red and some become white dwarfs
and some collapse to form black holes.
And if our knowing how
expanding and thus cooling space,
against all likelihood,
could lead us here, knowing we know, and now
could serve the needed good
of consolation for our voices
lingering merely as a puff

that lifts a candle flame,
then rousing consolation might aspire
        to praise this curse of consciousness,
this leap miraculous of neurons past
        synaptic clefts, this hidden fire,
no matter what thought must demand we know:
        the emptying of all we cherish,
            waste of all we sow,
here at the end, yet just the human end,
before we are resolved into the heavy elements
        from which we came, before we are,
            what once we were,
the undeliberated shining of a star.

THE SNOWY OWL

To merge his shadow with the moonlit earth,
the snowy owl shakes out his wings, sharp fire
from his first father in his opal eyes;
his croak pierces the January air
across the frozen field, over the water
steaming in the stream among the tamaracks.

And as I join him in the tamaracks—
which in my mind retain their autumn fire
although their needles smolder in the earth—
their stiffened branches quiver the cold air
that with each swirl of wind lashes my eyes.
These are my unlamenting tears, just water

meaning only what it's always meant for water
to find shape in what it occupies on earth—
a cheek's slope or a bed of rocks, as fire
must find its shape within itself, as air,
wishing to speak, defines the tamaracks
as border for the snowy owl's curved eyes.

And in my mind his eyes become my eyes
as I hunch down, framed by the tamaracks,
or float out on wet wind over the earth
in search of warmth that moves, feeling the air
buoyant beneath my gliding wings, like water
riding its tide, like fire balancing fire

on its blue heart. This is my father's fire
rising as fire always must rise from earth;
this, as it's always been, my father's water
changing to remain itself, secure as air
that brightens at brushed tips of tamaracks
the way eyes brighten in desire, the way eyes

widen when they meet the stare of other eyes.
And now I see upon the stirring earth
flashed multitudes of eyes glare back their fire:
I see them flame as moonlight flecks the water;
I see them down the pathways of the air;
I see their opal shining in the tamaracks.

My croak streaks *krow-rick* from the tamaracks
as I float there, my father's moonlight in my eyes,
and, ah, I can call *water,* I call *earth,*
I summon *fire,* I measure out the *air.*

CHAMP

The earliest recorded citing
dates back to the year 1609.
    Two centuries go by
    before a Captain Crum, one morning,
at a distance of 200 yards,
    conjectures I must be
187 feet from nose to tip of tail,
    and estimates I hold my head
at fifteen feet above the water line,
    possessing just three teeth,
two in the center, one set in my upper jaw;
    he sees a white star on my forehead
and a belt of red around my neck.
    But you're more disciplined
    at observation now,
    so now you know it's likely I'm
a good deal shorter than the first reports,
    and that I have a normal
    (for a monster) set of teeth,
    that probably the brave,
flamboyant red band sketched around my neck
    was just a trick of liquid light-
the early sun reflected off a sliding wave.
    You know now I could be
the lost descendant of a plesiosaur,
    considered by the skeptical
to be extinct for 60 million years,
    which sometimes grew past fifty feet,
    propelled itself with flippers,
had a small head on a slim, giraffelike neck.
    No longer native to the sea,
in order to survive in Lake Champlain,
    I must, as you now know,
    have taken on some recent features
    of warm-bloodedness

or learned to hibernate beneath the mud
    as in some local sense
  all us year-round Vermonters do.
Some day I may evolve the eloquence
  that will allow me to express
     how much it pleases me
  to be remembered, thought about,
even when not quite rightly understood.
    This keeps my spirits up,
so I'm delighted when you speculate
  that I might be a Zeugladon—
    a snakelike whale, extinct
  for 20 million years, who needs air,
    catches fish, and sleeps
with just his snout, which might look like a rock,
  above the surface of the lake.
    So far, there's only one
  half-decent photograph of me,
although a lawyer from Winooski and
    his social-worker wife,
  saw me up close, but never told
     the Champ Society
for fear their reputations would be ruined;
     and yet in 1982
  a law was passed protecting me,
    as an endangered species,
  from all hunting and from harm.
    The "Champ Identikit"
describes my personality
as "shy, elusive, curious"—quite true,
  but I have other moods as well,
    as when at dusk the lights
  along the shore, that were not there
just several centuries ago, flash on
    like melancholy stars,
each with a rainbow aura of its own,
  and make me wish I could approach
you where you are and let myself be known.

But I must tell you now:
my real name isn't Champ, though I don't mind
if you prefer to call me that;
I only want to say,
watch for the white star on my head,
the red band on my neck.
I think you'd miss me if I went away.

LANDSCAPE GOAT

I'm not to blame—this poem about a goat
    may not mean what it says
it means. The lake I walk beside, along
      a willow row that leads
down to a waterfall beside a cave,
        might be a city street
    if you construe that my depicting
      such a country scene
conceals my bruising childhood in the Bronx.
        You might assume
    that my composing such a lake,
      which I forgot to say
    displays a family of ducks
drifting in harmony along one bank,
      means I'm repressing how
    my speechless father died or why
my mother's words could not reach down to where
    his buried understanding lay,
and this interpretation might appeal
    to some familiar need in you.
I also meant to mention there were bats
      inside that swirling cave—
    a sign, perhaps, of hidden thoughts;
when I was four one bit me on the arm,
    although, to tell the truth,
that memory is vague, and I suspect
    it may have been my brother who
      got bitten on the butt—
a comic touch for a pastoral poem!
    The row of willow trees might mean—
    though I have no wish to
usurp your role as my interpreter—
    something my landscape wants to say
      of sorrow that can't manage
to express its heart in any other way because,
    unlike reflections in a lake,

it can't confront itself.
And yet my saying this to you
might seem to indicate the opposite.
Who knows? for at this point,
I can't tell what I'd make of your reply,
how my interpretation would
interpret your interpretation of
this country scene, which does depict
a browsing goat and means
what sunlight on a lake can mean.
I'm sure at least I have
succeeded in communicating that
I can't communicate, although
if you'll resist your impulse to rewrite my poem,
no doubt to get my goat,
and thus not conjure garbage bags piled up
along a city street,
you'll see the lake; you'll see the ducks
who have by now moved out
from underneath the willows' shade;
you'll watch the goat interrogate the wind;
you'll hear the waterfall,
its flute-notes as it scales the rocks;
you'll look into the darkness of the cave
and hear my brother scream
as that mad bat—which keeps on coming back—
a grin upon its face,
refuses to release his butt,
which by now I associate with yours.
And if it saddens you
to think that what you make of me, my poem,
is all that you can know,
consider how the lake will look
when it is frozen fast and all the willow trees
are laden under silent snow.

IT WOULD HAVE BEEN ENOUGH

If only daffodils had caught the light,
   that would have been enough;
  and if to add variety,
   just crocuses and tulips
 splashed their colors in the dawn,
   that, too, would have sufficed;
  and if just sparrows, common sparrows,
not white-throated, dusky-evening, golden-crowned,
  had tilted on a limber bough
amid the silver smooth and silver rough
   and twined their whistlings in the leaves,
   that would have been enough.
To add variety, it would have been enough
   if only chickadees,
  the plain gray junco, and the nuthatch
also frequented the maple tree and played
   upon a puff of wind,
and, certainly, it would have been sufficient
  if, beside the steady maple,
for the sake of contrast in the hazy rain,
   a clump of gleaming birches swayed.
It would have been sufficient for variety
   without the tamaracks,
  without the pines, without the firs,
without the hemlocks harboring the wind;
   it would have been enough
to have the chipmunk pausing on his log
   without the browsing deer
who, one by one by one, their white tails flashing,
  leap across the minnow stream.
   We didn't need that much
  to want to make ourselves at home
   and build our dwellings here-
just light upon the lake would have sufficed to see,
   just changing light at evening
on a birch clump or a single maple tree.

For us to make ourselves at home,
             it would have been enough
if only we had said, "This is enough,"
             and for variety,
it would have been sufficient if we said,
             "This surely will suffice;'"
and when dawn brushed its shadows in the apple tree,
             if we had only said,
"How bountiful those shaded circles are,
             how silently they pull
      themselves together toward the stem,"
that bounty would have seemed more bountiful.
             And even now, if I should say,
"How bountiful," then just one daffodil,
      a single daffodil unfolding
             in a yellow vase
upon a maple table in the breeding sun,
             would be enough
      and seem abundant far beyond
what was sufficient to desire, except
             for one brown, ordinary sparrow
             on my windowsill,
which I cannot resist including in this light,
nor can I leave out rows of cedars,
winding through the valley up the misted hill.

MOUNTAIN ASH WITHOUT CEDAR WAXWINGS

The likely last nostalgic warmth of autumn
      has gone by, the amber leaves
have fallen from the mountain ash, and still
        luminescent berries
    hold their positions on the chill,
stiff branches, clustered together like orange stars,
      because no cedar waxwing's come
        to stuff its horny mouth
        in preparation for
    its migratory journey south.
Listen! for I'm no longer sure I know
      what words can reach the words in you,
      though words have been my life,
no cedar waxwing's visited my tree
        four bleak falls in a row,
after a quarter of a century
        according to my watch,
    because their southern habitat
has been deforested at the dumbfounding rate
      of eighty-two square miles a day.
And watching their not dwelling here a while,
        watching the silent way
    the orange berries seem to cry out
for the yellow blur of flurried wings
        that gives the gaudy gold
    of autumn its autumnal burnishing,
        summons to memory
    the losses I could not have known
life on this planet would inflict on me.
      I knew I'd have to face my aging
        and my death, but not
the death of forests, not of oceans, not the air;
        I knew I'd lose my parents,
        lose unsuspecting friends,
    but not the bond that lets us share

consoling voices from the past,
not faith in our true mother tongue that seemed,
hardly a rhyme ago,
generative as April mist,
evocative as February snow.
But now, dishonored and demeaned,
language itself, like ravaged earth, betrays
its own betrayers who
betray the laughter Chaucer knew,
betray Shakespearean remorse, whose mind,
beyond all anger and all tears,
as breeding as the sun,
could empathize with everyone.
These are not losses of my own,
losses that I can bear,
my temporary life,
but loss of what I once thought permanent—
the woods, the oceans, and the air,
loss of the binding words
that mean the meanings their intenders meant.
Is it too late for me to say,
for better or for worse,
I feel as empty as my mountain ash
without the cedar waxwings here,
I feel the loss, wide as our universe,
of everything that I hold dear?

FATHERING THE MAP

In May of nineteen-hundred forty-two,
    my father's birthday gift to me
      was a long cardboard map,
extending from green England in the west,
    past purple Germany,
      beige Russia, east to red Japan.
We hung it in the basement playroom where
    I tended my aquariums
of turtles, salamanders, frogs, and kept
      my pen of flop-eared rabbits,
my wood hutch of guinea pigs who slept
      within my tended peace.
    My father's plan was that together
we would track the progress of the war.
    He bought a box of colored pins
to represent each country's tanks and troops
      so that we could "keep score"
of Allied victories, but I recall
      the black pins spreading out
      across two darkened continents.
By August, cricket calls contending in the night,
    my father's faulty health turned bad
      as German armies camped
beside the Volga river outside Stalingrad,
      and it occurred to me
for the first time that we might lose—
      that purposes beyond
my comprehension might have chosen us
      to know defeat: we Jews,
      even here in America,
would be exterminated when the Nazis came.
      In nineteen forty-five,
we moved because my father died: two strokes
      had left him speechless,
      though his eyes were still alive
      when I last sat with him.

I had to give my turtles to the zoo,
      my salamanders and my frogs,
my flop-eared rabbits and my guinea pigs,
        and every loss I knew
went with them as if loss could be restored
        in a protected place.
      The day the moving truck arrived,
I cleared our cluttered map, pin by cold pin,
      from yellow Naples up to Finland,
orange Normandy to rainbow-hued Berlin,
      but left it on the basement wall
        in case the kid who came
to live there in my house could find
some other use for it, some other game.
      But that was forty years ago.
        I never met the boy
who moved in after me, and I don't know
      what he did with our map—
perhaps his father threw it out, replaced
      it on the wall when we sent troops
to South Korea, or they might have traced
      the torrid Gaza wars
so they could bear and understand
      the unchanged passions of
the shifting borders of the Holy Land.
      Maybe the boy who moved in next
received a birthday map of the whole world—
      as if his father were to say:
        keep count of oil spills
and each rain forest, stripped of trees,
whose species we exterminate each day;
      remember the first covenant
        Jehovah made with Noah
following the flood: *Neither shall flesh*
      be cut off to destroy the earth.
      Maybe his father's eyes
were fresh with tears as if he meant
      to keep a vow: "Mute death

is unredeemable; I can't accept
  our breaking of the convenant."
    The map I'll leave my son
will look like moonlight seething on the sea—
  all blank but for a single pin
    to represent an ark,
in hope another covenant to save the earth
    may find words in the dark.

FROM
Minding the Sun
(1996)

☾

OBSERVER

Only a universe with an initial density exactly equal to critical density
would be capable both of engendering motherly stars and of lasting
long enough to provide a home for the nuclear, chemical, and biological
reactions required for life to subsist. . . . This 'fertile" density is the first
condition any universe must meet before it can hope to produce its own
observer.

—HUBERT REEVES, *The Hour of Our Delight*

Muse of the universe,
muse of mass-energy, I'd never known
critical density
is a conception that I need
to take personally:

force of initial thrust required
for fiery particles to be propelled
without collapsing back because
the pull of gravity
could halt expansion and prevent the laws

that govern simple cooling
from engendering enduring stars.
Through improvising time, .
mothering stars could then provide us
with a place where melody and rhyme,

in turn, would be conceived from
nuclear and chemical reactions,
from organic ooze.
I'd never known that metaphor
also required mothering so that deep blues

can represent our gloom,
green can convey renewal, red evoke desire,
and white betoken emptiness
or innocence because those primal particles
designed us to express

what our initiating species has become—
observers of the patient stars
that mothered us to bear
true witness to the story of the past
unfolding everywhere,

enabling us to apprehend the music
of the whirling planets
as they orbited the sun,
enabling us to feel the harmony
fertile density had begun.

So here we are, observing with our eyes
the slant light through the pines
before the orange sun descends
behind the bluish-purple misted hills;
and here we are as moonlight sends

fresh flashings through the lake
and multiplies the silvery reflections
while they slide and spill
and merge with our own thoughts
which cast their own reflecting light at will

as if the act of looking
added hue and aura to the night;
and here we are at dawn, here's why we came,
observing with our ears
the way the whip-poor-will repeats his name,

hearing the pulse of words
we have evolved to listen with,
observing with the mind
the mind's brave observations of itself,
enabling us to find

thought can engender from its own
critical density
a fertile universe through which to roam,
which metaphor, in blue or green
or red or white, can designate as home.

THE LOSS OF ESTRUS

Estrus must have been lost at some point in human ancestry. . . . When hunting became a dominant male economic activity, perhaps the costs (in terms of fitness) to females !if constant sexual activity [due to the loss of estrus] were outweighed by the benefits !if receiving meat.

—DONALD SYMONS, *The Evolution of Human Sexuality*

Fertility is good—
I want to multiply, and yet
without that fabled loss of estrus, dear,
the wisdom of ancestral genes,
we'd now be making love just once a year.
That really would be quite enough,
assuming I could get the timing right,
unaided by the scent
of ovulation in the air,
if replication of myself were all sex meant
to me as a progenitor—just
an afternoon's hiatus from the hunt.
I don't know what the cost
to you has been, but you look mighty fit to me,
so I'll assume no zest is lost
in all our huff-and-puffing,
spendthrift, sexual activity
the loss of estrus—quite
untypical of mammals—made
inevitable. Thus, establishing the right
incentive for us males
to stick around, abandoned estrus set the stage
for the invention of
a marital ideal of love
around the seasons.
And more virtues
followed from the first:
as when one genius simian
woke up and understood

that a connection could be found between
his fornicating and his fatherhood.
Nuzzling his nervous wife,
he swore, "I'll bring meat home, my dear,
after our band completes the hunt; I vow
that I'll stay faithful through this year
and faithful when our kids
leave home, and if familiar shadows
gliding through my silent dreams are true,
even beyond the cramped-in grave
I'll rise to spend eternity with you."
And so it must have been
with that light, evolutionary leap
in self-persuading eloquence,
the world's first marriage vow was born;
that's why it still makes sense
for us to look each other in the eye and say
we'll redesign the creatures
that we are so we'll behave a better way
than any mammal has before.
Despite your ancestor's low motive for romance,
my dear, *protein deficiency*,
we'll now pretend the loss of estrus was
your own transfiguring idea
that captivated me,
an idea that new vows of love
might yet be built upon,
when my hot tooth for hunting flesh has cooled
and all hormonal scents are gone.

LAMENT OF THE MALE GAMETE

Throughout animals and plants: the sex cells or "gametes" of males are much smaller and more numerous than the gametes of females. . . . This places a limit on the number of children a female can have. . . . Since she starts by investing more than the male, in the form of her large, food-rich eggs, a mother stands to lose more if the child dies than the father does.

          —RICHARD DAWKINS, *The Selfish Gene*

Now, I suspect, she's learned to be on guard!
The gateway to the promised land
has been sealed off; I'm barred from entering.
The writing on the wall proclaims—
"Abandon hope all ye who fumble here!"—
and with these words that burn
into the echo cavern of my mind,
my dread of barrenness returns;
I shudder in the tumbling
of the crowded tide. Millions of years
conspired to make me small for speed,
so I could thrash and swim without the fears
of failure and of waste,
willing to brave fantastic odds.
But now heroic effort is in vain—
no force of mine can pierce this wall;
I feel unprecedented pain
in being cheated of the chance
to make myself into a multitude
because my scent of her
that once unfailingly could seek her out,
diminishes and fades.
I'm left with just a swimmer's urge
among massed millions of competitors
to stay afloat and bob about.
Yet I believe if I could merge
with her vast body, bountiful with food,

unite with her alone,
I would remain with her, protect our brood,
few though they are—unlike
the stars reflected on the sea.
Blind thrashing can't be all:
a mission to oblivion! There's got to be
a hidden passage through this wall
to where she waits for me.
My bruised head must be more than some grim sign
of her newfangled wish:
retaliation for old eons
of my kind deserting her.
I need new inspiration to go on,
bounce back and try again,
to keep my head above the tide,
triumphantly survive,
like trilobites evolved to fish,
like fish evolved to birds,
like birds reformed to glowing men
of bodily perfection and ordained,
cell by redeemed immortal cell,
to enter paradise.
Now with the tide receding, I foretell
I'll never reach my goal,
although I still cannot conceive
that nothing living will descend from me.
Through all the spume and roll
and slashing of the unrelenting waves,
I hear a drowning fellow call:
"We are such stuff as dreams are made on" and
I know at last that loss is all.

THE BARBER OF CIVILITY

We are asked to swallow a story about a village and a man in it who shaves all and only those men who [according to Lord Bertrand Russell's paradox] do not shave themselves. Grant this and we end up saying, absurdly, that the barber shaves himself if and only he does not. The proper conclusion to draw is just that there is no such barber.

—W.V.O. QUINE, *The Ways of Paradox*

Wishing to study the effects
of bafflement, to see
if metaphysical uncertainty depressed
or entertained a trusting mind, .
Lord Russell's ghost appeared one night to test
old Samson Horn, the tuneful barber
in my town, with his prize paradox:
"Let's say a barber shaves all men
who do not shave themselves;
accepting this, the problem for you, then,
is to decide if you're allowed,
according to these rules, to shave yourself."
Old Samson took these rules to heart,
for one can't have, he reasoned,
marriage, friendship, sports, or art
without constraining forms;
yet opposite conclusions seemed to him
logically inescapable,
nor was this splitting hairs—for if a barber
does not shave himself, the full
import of his not doing so is that
he's bound to shave himself;
and if he shaves before it's time for bed,
the rules do not permit
his taking scissors to his head.
Old Samson called and woke me from a nap
to cancel my appointment since

he could no longer work until he figured out
what this strange civil war
in his divided soul was all about,
although an operatic joy
swelled up in him when logic
spurned itself—as if the world we see
will not allow our words
to penetrate its silent mystery.
Samson closed down his barbershop
in the abandoned mill,
and vanished with his cats and dogs,
though I can see him still,
his scissors poised above my head,
until a snip achieved perfection worthy
of a Michelangelo.
And I have kept my vow
from snow to rain and rain again to snow
that I won't shave till he returns;
I walk the bridge as misty dawn swirls in,
and wonder if he took
the ghost to be a sign that he begin
another life in which
it's possible to shave and not to shave at once,
to stay and to depart,
to feel compassion with the mind
and follow algorithms with the heart.
My beard is now so long
that friends suspect some crisis changed
my image of myself, but that's absurd—
although, on the warped barber sign,
look there! I see Lord Russell's ghost transformed
into a luminescent bird.

PICNIC WITH PARADOX

Let me assume, my dear, that justice will
be done in the next life,
that what I suffer here in this polluted
world will be rewarded with
abundant compensating bliss
of my own choosing—
whether food or sex or walks
beside a silver stream, identifying birds,
or philosophic talks
with God, who also loves a paradox.
But if I know for sure
that justice triumphs in the end,
despite our human wars;
despite betrayals and the loss
of animals and trees and parents, friends,
then that benign belief
should bring me happiness in life and send
my wishes back to where I am,
content in this bereaving world. Yet if
I'm happy in this life
because I think that I'll be happy in the next,
I won't, according to the rules
of my own guiding text,
still qualify for compensating bliss
in paradise: for champagne picnics
with slow kisses in a clover field,
and thus without eternity
to hopefully anticipate, I'm trapped
again in mortal misery.
It seems my faith that compensating justice
will be done is only true
if I believe it's false,
and if I still believe it's true—
a prophecy that floods me now with joy
that I can share with you—
then justice, in effect, already

has been done on earth,
and you and I can stroll along
some clear June day beside a dwindling stream,
a picnic basket on my arm,
young, confident, and strong,
no need to fantasize or dream
as my uncontemplating body savors
its own sun-warmed ecstasy.
But that depicted youthful me is not
now who I am; that me is as
remote as paradise hypothesized,
and you, how clearly I can see
your vanished radiance
that once made my unwary body
blissfully oblivious
to anyone's distracting paradox.
There was no need then to think
there might come a day
when I'd be strolling by a silver stream,
discussing justice with a god
who oversees the way
we struggle to make sense of suffering
or finally allows our memories to fade
until thought is a glimpsed white bird
that disappears into the leafy shade
without a lilting melody
to recognize him by,
without a hopeful word, without a cry.

THE TREES WILL DIE

An increase of one degree in average temperature moves the climatic
zones thirty-five to fifty miles north. . . . The trees will die. Consider
nothing more than that-just that the trees will die.

—BILL McKIBBEN, *The End of Nature*

In lush Vermont let me consider
some familiar trees I've lived among
for thirty years of sleet and snow,
of sun and rain: the aspens
quaking silver when the wet winds blow,

the white oaks, with their seven-lobed leaves
and gently furrowed bark,
whose April buds sprout reddish-brown;
and I'll consider pin oaks,
their stiff branches sloping down

asserting their own space, and sculpted leaves,
flaming vermilion in the fall,
holding on even when they're curled and dry,
through freezing winter storms
in which we huddle, you and I,

around a fire that woos us back to feel
what our ancestors felt
some sixty-thousand years ago;
and I'll consider red oaks with their pointed leaves,
shiny dark trunks that seem to know

the secret of slow growth,
a message safe to pass along.
And then, considering the plenitude
of maples here, I'll start with sugar
for its syrup and its symmetry, its brood

of tiny yellow flower clusters
in the spring, and in the autumn such a blaze
of orange, gold, and red,
whatever gloom might form the drizzling weather
in my doom-reflecting head,

relief comes from the self-forgetfulness
of looking at what's there—
the trees, the multitude of trees.
I stop here to consider in the brief years left
to praise them and to please

you who have loved their scented shade,
their oceanic choiring in the wind. And so I'll list
a few more that I know:
the silver maple and the willow and the birch,
box elder, basswood, and the shadblow

whose pinkish-white flowers
quicken the awakened woods
and quicken me. And then the spruce and pines,
their slender, tapered cones
glimmering intricate designs

that tempt astonished eyes to contemplate
how an indifferent force—
just evolutionary randomness,
yet so like old divinity—
could wrest such pattern from initial emptiness.

Before our history began,
the void commanded
there be congregated trees and creatures filled
with words to mimic them
and represent the moods that spilled

out of the creature's thoughts into the world
so that the trees and names for trees
would then be joined as one:
the melancholy hemlocks in the humming dark,
the tamaracks which flare gold in the sun

as if to hold the light
of wavering October in their arms
a little longer, as I do—
yet though they're evergreens at heart,
like me, my dear, and you,

they lose their needles when the cold comes on.
And as the tilted planet turns
to offer us fresh colors that embellish speech,
more names rush into view:
the sycamore, the cedar, and the beech,

horse chestnut, butternut,
the hickories, black walnut, and of course
the cornucopia of fruits—
apple and cherry, pear and plum and peach—
each with a tang that suits

the palate of whatever taste
one might have dreamed of ripened paradise.
When I consider how
a man-made shift in climate of a few degrees
reveals the rebel power we now

have learned to cultivate
in order to subdue the animals
and take dominion, like a curse,
over the fields, the forests, and the atmosphere—
as if the universe

belongs to us alone—I wonder
if consideration of the family of trees
might give us pause
and let us once again obey the sun
whose light commands our human laws.

FROM
Rounding It Out
(1999)

☾

AUBADE

Our sun has left just half its life to spill—
About five billion years before it must
Explode, collapse upon itself, and will
Back to the universe its final thrust
Of heat we creatures long have counted on.
Waking warm here in bed, we trust
This light to help imagine when light will be gone
About five billion years from now, it must
Experience diminishment,
As must we, too, as must we all.
Observers, we can find our last content
In comprehension that the fall
Of yellow petals on our window sill,
Like little suns, is what we have to will,
A melody to whistle in the dawn.
Our sun has left just half its life to spill.

APRIL DAWN

I sing my hungering for green as if I could
Make April luminously greener through
My surging with the sap-inspired wood,
My ice-locked spirit leaping up into
The sun-splashed, hawk-encircled air
As valley vistas blazing in their dew,
Receding and advancing everywhere,
Make April luminously greener through
Dawn's bold unfolded doubling in my sight,
Which knows all dawns like this I've felt before
Because the green I am now singing might
Be everybody's green—it could be your
Repeat reflection on the not yet quite
Completed life we've shared, with more
Loss left to come, more hawk-flight left unseen,
Still hungering for green, more April green.

LATE SUMMER PURPLE

Wild aster, bee balm, phlox, chrysanthemum
Proclaim pure purple in the pallid dawn,
Asserting there's more blossoming to come,
More purple in the prickling thistle thorn,
More purple in the valley's swirling haze;
Even the robin's shadow on the lawn,
Even your welcome of the dwindling days
Proclaim pure purple in the pallid dawn.
Pure purple is the color of your need
To have your mood made manifest, your final flair
Before October's culminating leaves exceed
In parting opulence the purple air
That radiates about your head
As if dispensing rapture everywhere
You move to make a purple hymn to hum:
Wild aster, bee balm, phlox, chrysanthemum.

RIPENESS

Familiar summer now seems strangely new
As this faint chill of languid August dawn
Shivers the clustered berries in the dew
As if completed ripeness has been born
From ripeness recollected ripening.
Ripeness again repeated, here and gone,
Presence and .loss together as both bring
A scented chill to languid August dawn.
Five billion years of evolution on our earth
Produced this momentary ripeness in the sun,
This rounded revelation at the birth
Of sweet acceptance in the fruitful one
Prolific meaning earth can offer you,
Ripeness to smell, to taste, to meditate upon,
Red raspberries becoming redder in your view
Which makes familiar summer strangely new.

PREGNANT GOAT

Aware that I am here observing her,
The pregnant, brown goat browsing in that field
Now pauses at her chewing as the whir
Of swallows swooping from the barn, the peal
And splatter of their twitterings, accompany
Wild flapping of her ears, although
From my side of the road, how can I know
If the connections I see she can see?
The pregnant, brown goat browsing in that field
Appears serene to me; perhaps it's true
She takes raw pleasure in the pleasure yield
That I conceive from watching her, as if she knew
She has more life inside her life, more time,
As she seems roused to feel the stir
Of her slow browsing in my blood when I'm
Aware that I am here observing her.

WATERFALL

You cup the leaping water in both hands,
Kneeling beside the spurning waterfall,
And what your untried body understands,
Poised in pure receptivity, is all
That childhood can allow, sensation so
Harmonious—the stream, the flute-trill call
Of orioles—you know by knowing not to know,
Kneeling beside the spuming waterfall.
And I can merge with you but only by
Withholding what this father wishes most—
To touch, to keep, as if by touching I
Might pour out of myself, a ghost
Of foam and spray, a floating shade who has
New spuming flow to voice my soft demands.
But no, I have no touch to keep you as
You cup the leaping water in both hands.

OCTOBER MAPLES

No wind at all, late golden maples glow
Silent and still in bold October sun,
And I, contained within their aura, know
Their luminescent stillness to the bone, at one
With silence made articulate as light,
At one with your own oneness even though
I see myself dissolving in your sight.
Silent and still in bold October sun,
The windless lake reflects the maples' glow,
And I—as if my mind becomes the lake—
Know only what its open waters know,
The oneness of its give and take
Of noonday light; passing October pauses
On the lake of my still mind, without a cause,
And where there stirs no fluting sound, no flow,
No wind at all, late golden maples glow.

BALED HAY

Wheels of baled hay bask in October sun:
Gold circles strewn across the sloping field,
They seem arranged as if each one
Has found its place; together they appeal
To some glimpsed order in my mind
Preceding my chance to pause here—
A randomness that also seems designed.
Gold circles strewn across the sloping field
Evoke a silence deep as my deep fear
Of emptiness; I feel the scene requires
A listener who can respond with words, yet who
Prolongs the silence that I still desire,
Relieved as clacking crows come flashing through
Whose blackness shows chance radiance of fire.
Yet stillness in the field remains for everyone:
Wheels of baled hay bask in October sun.

BODY PRAISE

Meanwhile I'll celebrate my body's parts,
The noble nose that boldly leads the way,
Gray eyes that glisten with seduction's art,
The mouth whose smile tilts subtly on display,
For what am I if not the aggregate
Of my proud appetites, the nervous leap
Of gossip from each synapse to relate
Its story to the neural neighborhood and keep
The noble nose that boldly leads the way
Directed toward a transcendental goal
To justify pained searching some redeeming day.
So thanks, dumb feet, thighs, genitals, you all
Have something to contribute, gut and heart,
And though you cannot glimpse beyond that wall
Where some great revelation starts,
I'll celebrate you, meanwhile, body parts.

LEAVES IN AUTUMN WIND

You need no meaning more than mindless leaves
That brush their reds and yellows in bright air
As if to specify an image there
Whose disappearance can be rendered permanent;
Thus with their vanishing contained, you grieve
So quietly that it might seem you spent
Whatever sorrow might inform the scene,
Leaves brushing reds and yellows in bright air,
On finding meaning merely in what colors mean.
I still can see you underneath a tree,
Your hands outstretched to catch more evening light,
Though maybe in your mind you're watching me,
And maybe meaning means no more than sight
Can cherish, and in cherishing let be,
So that your silent minding heart believes
You need no meaning more than mindless leaves.

THE AFTERMATH

Nothing remains except the aftermath—
Odor of rain, now that the valley air is dry,
A hint of whispering along the forest path
That we once wandered through here, you and I,
As if past presence lingers through the pantomime
Of muted loss, rehearsals of good-bye
With more ongoing aftermath to come:
Odor of rain, now that the valley air is dry.
And if no one returns to realize
That we are gone, and no one anywhere—
On hearing how the startled blackbird cries—
Can conjure our late absence waiting there
From the light scent left over from the storm,
Who will distinguish in mild evening air
Cosmic indifference from cosmic wrath?
Nothing remains except the aftermath.

LEAVE TAKING

So good-bye body, good-bye universe,
Its nearing time to take your leave of me,
Although desire's not spent yet to converse
With you, nor lost its curiosity
About your chance appearance on the cosmic scene
Or how complex became complexity,
Whose meaning meant what need contrived to mean
In time to take untimely leave of me.
Can solace yet be found for one who grieves
A father lost, a mother vanishing,
In just low oceanic choiring of blown leaves,
Encounters of a swallow's wing
With orange evening light, no more, no less?
Yes, there's sufficient reason still to sing
A rounded song for better or for worse,
So good-bye body, good-bye universe.

NOCTURNE

How little separates me from the night:
My moist breath merges with the moistened air;
From my cupped hands a flutter of reflected light
Ascends as if a bird had been enfolded there—
A gathered whiteness that can fly
My message of replenished care,
My offer to the dark, my sole reply.
My moist breath merges with the moistened air,
Summons to its blurred self what waits beyond,
Projects its own illumination to
Moon-laden branches by the frozen pond,
To cavern icicles our awed ancestors knew.
I see how cloudy indivisibility
Divides, how whirled division mists to white;
I recognize lulled voices calling me,
How little separates me from the night.

FROM
Elk in Winter
(2004)

☾

LATE IN THE ROCKIES

Here in the Rockies as dark clouds descend,
Gray sky and snow upon the peaks contend and merge,
Partaking of each other's shadows in the lake
Where sleek ducks circle and then separate;
Their luminescent wings reflect

Bright breaks in the black clouds, and I forget
Why lately I moved here. In this new place
I can reflect on what I see in the still lake,
The reassembling ducks, called goldeneye, that merge
White wings with snowy sky, so I can't separate

These swirling whitenesses
Or tell this house from rooms I won't forget.
The whirling seasons merge
In just a single image in the lake—
The gold eye of a duck—which like gold sky

Between black clouds reflects
My eye as one still image on the lake.
And now I have no need to separate
Sorrows of empty doors I can't forget
From vistas darkening—all merge,

Merely by being gone, into a white glow
On a lake where rowing with my father
I reflect my rowing with my son,
For I forget which day is which;
I cannot separate lake shimmer

From gold light spans in the sky. And staring up
Between dark closing clouds, I can forget
Why I can't separate
Where we were coming from or rowing to—they merge,
Just as a duck's eye can reflect my own.

Now only the closed sky is home.
Ducks on the lake reflect themselves, and yet
Their shadows merge with doorway shadows
And with windows glistening
That I have still forgotten to forget.

DEER AT THE GARDEN

Even asleep, I hear them stirring in the woods,
Restless like me, and hungry,
Their large ears alert to danger sounds, human,
Or merely wind, though since there never is enough
To eat, they'll trample down my garden
And devour what's mine. True, they're just deer,

But when I watch their eyes, I don't see deer
As creatures with no rights, enough
Of them already in the woods,
I see what they would feel if human
Understanding told them I was hungry,
That the purpose of a garden

Is to fence those out who failed to make a garden
Though their children, just like deer,
Through no fault of their own, also are hungry.
I'm not to blame, and I reject that human
Sentiment, because there's not enough
Where many people live, the same as in the woods,

As fear too is the same within the woods
Or out, and since I can't help everyone, it's human
That I first take care my children not go hungry
And can sleep at ease within my garden,
Though they seem wary just like deer
When I gaze in their eyes. It's good enough

If I can keep them safe; it's good enough
If I can keep my garden
Flourishing while more and more gaunt deer
Keep coming from the woods,
And though their limpid eyes look human,
Don't blame me because they're hungry.

Don't blame me that people too go hungry
For there's only so much room within a garden
Whether filled with people or with deer,
Some must make do within the woods
Where there can never be enough,
Though knowing that can cause more human

Misery. Hungry at heart for there to be enough
In all those teeming gardens and lush woods—
Are we most human when we see ourselves as deer?

WHITE HORSE

There in the middle distance in a field
Surrounded by a sagging fence,
A white horse canters head-up with an ease
Suggesting that he thinks he's beautiful.
On the south border, stacked between two trees,
A year's supply of split wood waits,
And from the north a stream runs toward me
Where it feeds a large trout pond
In which the white horse is reflected
When he drinks, his neck bowed in an arc.

From where I watch, among dark firs,
Upon an elevation of my own,
I see the streaking whiteness of the horse;
I see the Mission mountain range,
Its chiseled peaks across the broadened sky
Already glistening with early snow,
As if a theme had been expanded
To a magnitude beyond what meditation
Might have thought impossible.

Let light, I say out loud to no one
But myself, illumination of the scene
And of my mind, become a theme
That out of need I make my own:
The white horse in the field, the vast white
Of the mountain range, the spawning pond
Now shimmering in midday sun
With white wings on its coasting ducks;
Let them reveal nothing but what they are,
Horse, mountain, pond, without purpose,
Without meaning, without hope; yet let them join
In one white theme because I will it so.

Horse, mountaintop, the leaping trout,
All share the mirrored light as if
Their flashing whiteness can compose the scene,
Can gather it together so a horse,
Poised in the arc its bowed head makes,

Might mean more than in fact it does,
As if somehow translucent consciousness
Really were part of a design
In which the flow of undulating light,
Whiteness connecting everything I see,
Were not my own invention out of need.
           What need? What am I saying here
That does not falsify the scene itself
With hinting impositions of my own?
Only horse, mountain, pond, the silent ducks,
Each in its lone existence separate
From mine, actually dwell there,
And yet shared whiteness, which my mind
Construes as part of a design, shines forth
In this suspended moment when I can believe,
With that horse stationary in the field,
All whiteness in the world is beautiful.

ELK IN WINTER

Laden with snow
    the moonlit high pines
Loom above their shadows
    in the undulating drifts,
And in the watcher's mind
    a strange serenity
Pervades the silence
    of the windless scene,
As if permanent winter seals the woods
    from further change
And sets the mood the watcher now
    considers his reward
For seeing rounded moonlit forms
    with luminescent curves
And sweeping shades of blue.
    As silence deepens
Into deeper thought, the watcher,
    unresistant to the spell
His watching adds to the still woods,
    hears footfalls softly
Crunching in the shadowed snow,
    step upon sure unhurried step,
As marching elk, perhaps a hundred
    in a staggered line,
Their nostrils smoking over glowing eyes,
    push through on an ancestral path
to where elk go in wintertime
    beyond the watcher's gaze.
The watcher sees the elk as a tableaux,
    held in abeyance in his mind,
Because he senses some vague correspondence
    in their unrushed passing
Through the shadows of the pines
    and his hushed witness to the scene,
As if he could be anyone who came upon
    tall elk in moonlight,

Moving beneath loose shades of evergreens.
      And yet the watcher must
Acknowledge that awareness
      of a half-formed wish
to dwell forever in his watcher's mood
      distracts him into reverie
And thus disturbs his merging
      with the moonlit atmosphere
So that the silver scene can have
      no correspondence to himself
Other than that strong stomping elk
      have somewhere else to go
And feel no haste in getting there.
      He ponders that the wish
to lose himself in thinking of the passing elk
      defeats its goal
By mirroring his roused and wishful self
      and thus revives the gloom
Of contemplating his own murmured life
      or what is left of it.
His life, his self-reflecting life,
      with children gone into another mist,
And parents having crossed
      the last shore of the roaring brink,
Is it too precious to be dwelt upon
      with all his ghosts now
Numbered in the name of loss?
      The shudder of that thought
Flows backwards and recedes, and now
      the last of the cascading elk,
In what had seemed an endless line,
      passes from view;
The watcher sees himself
      beneath a steadfast tree,
His face in moonlight almost featureless,
      despite its worn-out care,
And does not know how long in silence
      he's been standing there.

TWIN POEM

Here is a poem about my fated brother
Who did not get born, a poem about
Our father's death in one swift stroke
And mother's rushed remarriage
To an evasive, melancholy man.

And yet my twin continues in my life
Whenever we converse within a poem
Because—as he once said—having
A sympathetic brother, one like me,
Helps him to realize what kind of man

He might have been despite our father's early death
And mother's sad remarriage to a man
Whose gloom went deeper than a poem
Can reach to cure, whose one defining truth
Was living death through dread of death.

Our father was a man without a twin
To ease his pain, nor could he talk of things
That might distract him from his fear of death—
Sights like the shadow of a solitary man
Strolling along a stony shore,

Whose liquid shade would be my brother
Out enjoying the soft evening air,
Reading a poem about a woman's loneliness
Walking beside a lake, feeling
Impersonal serenity, as any man

Can feel who steps outside himself. My twin,
Casting his shadow on the lakeside stones
There in the distance with the water birds,
Still shares my history: the truth
Of how a man can reinvent the vanished child

Bred by his parents' suffering.
In the extended sunset of my poem I can
Observe my shadow lengthen on the stones
And leap across the water to a cloud,
Grieved son that once I was, now a grown man.

WHAT WOULD WIND SAY?

Gathering grief has settled in my eyes,
    my body loses its solidity.
The lost past, like dense shade, drifts further still;
    where are my hours and days, where are they now?
Now soon enough I'll be with you, unrecognized;
    I'll wander down the dust
    without the ease of wandering.
What good to have a life set down in words?
    I pause at the sharp edge of what is sayable;
my friends reach out, but I'm not there;
    my enemies find me invisible.
I'm just an oboe played beneath a tree,
    a flute-note faint beyond a stream.
If I could find assertion in complaint,
    who'd listen; if I uttered out a curse,
    who would take heed?
Can reason talk one out of one's despair;
    can consolation be called forth
    and made obedient?
I'm glad the circling eagle has no use for me;
    the raven's raucous cry comes close enough;
the deer are curious, but not for long;
    the bear cubs keep the mother bear in sight;
    I'm brother to the bobcat and the owl.
Is it not totally astonishing
    that I take notice of myself? For what?
What would wild wind or rising water say
    were they, too, burdened
    with vain consciousness?
I make do with my making do,
    and for a moment I forget myself,
but then awareness, summoned not by me,
    returns of its own brute accord;
one thought of you—and you are gone again.
    Again you vanish, and now still again

what is not there is there as palpable
        as stone with etched-in words
        for some pale stranger passing by.
Your absence is as bright
        as sunlight on the sea,
illuminating the receding depths of air,
        blue fading into softer blue as if
some random thought of fading blue
        extended everywhere.

CONTENTMENT

This is the day I've waited for;
  The lion lies down with the lamb;
  And everything I was and am
Is ripe without desire for more.

Cruel eating ceases on this day;
  There is no hiding and no chase;
  Sufficient is the time and place
To be as if to be were play.

All lovers make a rightful pair;
  The child feels thanks with nothing owed
  For what the parents have bestowed.
A harvest blessing fills the air;

A breeze that first gave Adam breath
  When life was one with gratitude—
  A heartfelt thought, a worded mood
That had no argument with death.

The stream I chill to walk across
  Preserves each pebble in its voice;
  Its song has no idea of choice
Or change, and so it can't know loss.

It doesn't know it doesn't know
  And can't tell was from yet to come
  Or even where it started from;
There's only flow, there's only flow.

I've nothing further to discover;
  I shudder that I've dreamed it all-
  What follows after gaudy fall
When this awaited day is over.

GO JUMP

By Darwinian standards I am a horrible mistake . . . But I am happy to be voluntarily childless, ignoring the solemn imperative to spread my genes. And if my genes don't like it, they can go jump in the lake.

—STEVEN PINKER, *How the Mind Works*

Inspired by your "mistake," I'll ask my genes
To do the same. So, Steven, watch them race
Like kids along a dock, grab their rough knees,
Plunge in ass first. June heat provides this place

(Approved with my deliberate assent)
Beside a willow tree, for them to take
A holiday from replication's work,
Disturbing their reflections in the lake.

And thus I liberate myself to will
The self-willed life high thought aspires to live
While they are splashing in wild play,
Released from the solemn imperative

That kept me hot in sexual pursuits,
A robot driven proud by jealousy.
And while they frolic in fresh merriment,
I choose autonomous philosophy,

Unburdened of Darwinian desires,
And make peace with base instincts that have led
Me to the edge, emboldened by your book
That claims my mind has power to slay the dread

Old dragon of grim evolution's laws.
So when my genes return from their long swim,
Have dried their little backsides in the sun—
Fathered from leaping laughter at your whim—

What voluntary metaphor can you
In happiness paternally provide
To send them packing home inside my blood
Where lust and mirthless vanity reside?

RIPENESS

> Maybe before he wrote it down,
Shakespeare declaimed out loud,
> "Ripeness is all!" as if
for that immortal instant he inhabited a world
> of his own making. But
in that moment of his worded breath,
> one million billion billion atoms were
flung free into the universal air,
> and so the likelihood is that
I, here and now, must have inhaled
> a few of them, some dusty grains
of what great empathetic Shakespeare might
> have meant by ripeness, some
abundant season of the mind
> my straining mind
might name and harvest as its own.
> I know forgetfulness
won't qualify as ripeness:
> take my aged mother
who does not recall her husband died
> three years ago. And yet
my knowledge she no longer knows,
> yes, that might qualify,
my resolute awareness nothing
> can restore her sense of self
that once could contemplate
> the loved ones she had lost
and find black loss acceptable because—
> because no other choice
can maintain sanity. One can contrive,
> to take necessity
as if, to take possession of one's life,
> one willed oneself to will
each circumstance one suffered from.
> Like August drought

that desiccates the stunted fields
        and makes the forests tinder
for the unassuaging fires, Nature
        must have her wary—there is
no fruitful arguing with that, no matter
        how grim that may seem.
And yet I cannot help but feel
        true ripeness might connote
some sense of sweetened thought
        available to all, some atom
from the lexicon of what life's bounty gives
        and dying takes away,
Say like the *p* in ripeness or the *p*
        in Shakespeare's name,
the letter we might choose to signify
        prolific life— *p* as in peach,
or plum, or pear, or apricot,
        or apple with its double *ps*;
I've got a *p* in my name too. I watch
        my thoughts drill off
into an alphabet of wistfulness
        because I can't find ripeness
in my mother's deepening demise
        or my contrivance of necessity
redeemed as choice. And yet
        the overwhelming sweetness
of sweet Shakespeare's words,
        the mystery of what he meant,
lightens my mind and makes the lilting air
        although impersonal, still good
to grasp and gather in the lungs,
        so that it might appear
some plenitude of ripeness, even only
        of ripe words, might still
occur at any moment, anywhere.

FROM
Composing Voices
(2005)

☽

THE MARRIAGE MOOSE

Yes, I'm prepared to vow tomorrow on
our wedding day to cherish you until
I die, but wouldn't it, my dear, be much
more realistic if I only claim,
based on the up-to-date statistics, that
I will be faithful until some more youthful
damsel should one balmy day come strolling by?
Kidding—of course I'm only kidding—but
we can't control the future, we can't know
what motives drive somebody else's mind
no less our own. And yet I do believe
choice also can affect our destiny,
though not so much perhaps as accident.
        Pure chance is what inspired me to propose:
Surely you must recall, the two of us,
only a month or so after we'd met,
were hiking through the woods in Maine,
when suddenly a giant moose appeared
out from behind a stand of hemlock trees,
confronting us, lowering his antlers,
pawing the mush of moss and mashed-down leaves,
rolling his head with widened, glaring eyes.
        While clinging to each other, all we thought
to do was hide behind a tangled shrub
enveloped in the shade. Bone-shocking fear
was what we shared that day; nothing was said
and there was nothing else we could have done
but hope the snorting moose would not attack.
Could his moose-mind have speculated we,
entangled in each other's arms, were one—
a creature he had never seen before
and best be wary of? That anxious night
beside the fire when, impassioned, I
proposed to you without considering
how we'd support ourselves or what I'd do
as my life's work, something compelled me then—

and it was not just ordinary lust,
although, God knows, hot blood throbbed in my veins—
to want to make love permanent. Maybe
fear was a part of it, visceral fear
of transience, fear of our fragility
evoked by that encroaching moose. That moose,
that drooling moose, became my Muse incarnate,
thus inspiring in me promises
of loyalty with which I filled the air
in that reverberating forest night.
          Transfigured in my moonlit memory,
antlers diffused into a halo, eyes
set in a constellation of new stars,
the moose in misty spirit will attend
our ceremony of exchanging vows,
proclaiming Love's true triumph over time!
          And so, beyond dull reason, and beyond
what all the world's statistics say, I pledge
fidelity in light of an idea,
a lunatic idea of permanence,
as when, beside a fire ringed with stones,
recounting what we had not counted on—
a story to take with us on our way—
we offered up our thanks for help divine:
our blessed encounter with one baffled moose.

MONKEY EVOLUTION

First I'll describe what happened yesterday,
and then, my dear, I'll make my huge request.
After my guest appearance in her class
in which I argued most persuasively,
I must admit, that Darwin's bold idea,
Descent by Natural Selection, has
explanatory power no other theory
showing what we are can emulate,
Professor Dunn described her husband's job—
teaching Capuchin monkeys how to help
disabled people who can't use their hands,
bringing them water, answering the phone,
keeping them company. Across the hall
in the new lab, the monkey crouched upon
her husband's shoulder, bright-eyed, curious,
and then as I approached, she suddenly
leapt out toward me, entwined her skinny arms
around my neck and held me tight as if
she never would let go. Although surprised,
Professor Dunn's admiring husband said:
Like humans, monkeys also fall in love
irrationally at first sight, and I
was designated to be honored so.
        Deep in my mind I heard the surging swell
of Richard Wagner's masterful duet
when Tristan and Isolde, those lost lovers
in the dwindling night, wholly embrace
their single destiny. I blush to think
that I was flattered, and I wonder now
what wayward monkey intuition brought
her sudden passion on. She snatched the pen
from my shirt pocket and then raced away
while looking back to see if I would try
to follow and retrieve the pen back, laughing—
I'm sure that's what her chirping meant—as if
she knew love ought to end in play. Right then

I wanted a Capuchin of my own
and so I called our Vet to ask what is
involved in caring for a monkey pet.

He told me they are prone to catching cold,
that they are always bumping into things
and breaking bones. The greatest cause of death
in monkey ancestors, falling from trees,
he said, accounts for why the fear of falling
to this day still haunts our human dreams;
what's more, they never can be housebroken,
you have to diaper them throughout the day,
since, unlike wolves, monkeys evolved in trees,
so when they pooped the problem wasn't theirs,
they didn't have to learn to clean things up.

Consider this: owning a monkey is
like having a rambunctious two-year old
living forever in your house. You think
that even for the tender sake of love
you can contend with that? And now, my dear,
for my delayed request: I must confess
that I can't manage such a pet alone;
now that our kids are grown and gone,
now that the bloom of youth has left a pallor
in our cheeks, I need you to agree
that we'll adopt a monkey for our home.

A big advantage is you won't compete
for my attention or my loyalty,
not after all these operatic years.
Can you imagine that I'd love you less,
or that I'd ask for a divorce—a joke,
that's just a joke—should you reject me now?

STILL ON MY WAY

So I'll continue on my way, with your
good company, whoever you may be;
you'll get to know some of my other selves,
my cat, my dog, my monkey, my tame bear—
a yarmulke upon his comely head,
which he has grown accustomed to by now.
        Now let's imagine that you are my twin,
since, when one gets right down to it, there's little
to distinguish us (yet maybe that's
enough to cause much harm) and that includes
the animals; we eat, we shit, we make love,
suffer, and we die. And let's assume
that we are walking by a silver stream
in autumn when the modulating leaves,
though still abundant on the trees, display
extravagance so sumptuous that we
receive their colors almost as a gift,
almost as if they flourished toward their end
as compensation for our being here.
        My tame bear throws his shiny yarmulke
high in the whistling air to celebrate
his victory over his creaturehood,
though you, dear twin, may well suspect him for
some irreligious irony, despite
his rapt attention to the mystic way
the mellow colors merge and flair when touched
with intermittent light as a mild breeze
uplifts the nestled leaves and stirs the stream.
        But then a huge wind that's accompanied
by rain so thick that it obliterates
the cringing sky and floods the shore, raises
a wave that stirs to mud the riverbank
and of the muck creates a monster from
the sunken past, a beast whose face takes on
the features of whomever it devours:

a cat, a dog, a monkey, or a bear,
and even you when terror twists your mouth
into a mask I hardly recognize.
          I see his smoky eyes pursuing you,
my twin, and then I see you disappear
into the forest mist. I hear a pause,
whose blank duration I can't estimate,
before the mist evaporates and lets
the blazing disk of orange sun return
into the unobstructed sky; then I
am back where I had been before the storm
descended like an angry god, and, lo!,
I see the spinning yarmulke float down
and land on the bear's head where it belongs.
          I'm pretty sure that I've recorded this
as it occurred, although I may have left
some details out since memories are not
infallible and get mixed up with dreams.
Ah yes, I now recall (though maybe longing
is a factor here) the monkey snatched
away the yarmulke and climbed a tree,
and-someone who had not been there to watch
might find what happened next incredible—
the monkey spoke. He said: "I sure enjoy
your company, although I didn't know
at first whom I could trust, and I'm amazed
by human laughter, how it can reveal
and make incarnate longing to connect,
to bind what chance and time would separate,
that drives you and your brother on your way."

GRANDMA RECALLED

At my first Passover, Grandma proclaimed,
"My matzo balls are able to defy
the law of gravity, so eat them now
or else they'll float right off your plate. Last year
some stuck inside the chandelier—I had
to get a ladder from my neighbor's yard
so I could reach that high and scrape them off.
My recipe's a miracle—maybe
not equal to the Red Sea's parting so
we Jews could leave behind the yoke of our
Egyptian servitude, but it's a sign;
don't think God's not concerned with household things."

And now, my son, for your first Passover,
let me admit my childhood miracle
was that I gobbled down those matzo balls
and didn't die, although I still don't know
what purpose Yahweh spared me for, maybe
just to preserve important memories
that Grandma wanted me to share—like when
the Cossacks rode down from the roaring hills,
stole their fine jewelry and burned their homes.

They all escaped, bribing officials at
a border town, huddling and shivering
deep in an oceanic freighter's hold,
arriving in America where they
were free to buy and run a candy store—
a candy store—can you imagine that,
after what they had undergone, hiding
and sharing rationed portions of hard bread.

That's why you'll learn to eat your mother's
matzo balls tonight: to test your strength
for harder trials still to come—like those
inflicted by the Pharaoh in the past.
You're old enough right now to know
that there are people in the world that want
us all exterminated, blotted out;

that's how it is, that's how it was, that's how
forever it will be, unless Grandma,
busy as always up in paradise,
arranges for the Lord to intervene.
       The miracle of hers I liked the best
was that she made us laugh while lying there
right at the edge of death; I heard her tell
my mother she should have the windows washed,
since whether she recovered or did not,
there would be visitors parading through.
       Amused by her own joke, Grandma survived
for one more day, and when the neighbors came
to pay respects, there in the pantry stood
her matzo balls in rows of giant jars
ready to serve. And come indeed they did:
the baker brought us seeded rolls and cakes;
the grocer brought us carrots, beets, and greens;
the butcher brought us kosher sausages;
the mailman brought the paper with late news—
that Germany had just invaded France.
Did they teach you at school what happened next?
       I wonder now what Grandma knew up there
newly at home in distant paradise
with her adoring friends, how much bliss time—
eternity?—is needed to forget,
or can she still be cooking matzo balls?

FROM
Still Here, Still Now
(2008)

☾

ANOTHER MARCH

Another March, and in chilled trees thick sap
Begins to surge—a fact so fundamental I
Embrace its deep impersonality;
Yet it is I who feel it even though
I surely could be anyone. So, too,
Our life together, reaching back
A half a century, recaptures you
While planting daffodils in autumn mist,
Gleaming tomato stalks in May, as if
I read about us in a gilded book:
Our story's rounded with its end, just as
Returning seasons change and merge—
The thrum of summer I remember as
A hummingbird suspended at a rose—
Becoming one, as we are one, and full
With ripeness and with ruddy ripening,
Forever vanishing, forever there,
Forever gone and irreplaceable.

GRANDSON

His father piled the colored blocks
up to the level of his eyes, so he,
a force of Nature like a blast of wind,
could knock them down,
knowing his father right on clue
would build the tower up again
for him to scatter on the rug, as if
it represented the whole universe,
and yet without harm done. The blocks
seemed tumbled in perpetuity—
the future right before my eyes
to contemplate, for me,
the father of a father of a son.
          And he would turn his head
to make sure that I was observing him,
so that his laughter spanned
our generations there, spreading from him
to his observing father, then to me,
the father of a father of a son,
and back again, renewed, revitalized,
and ready to again move on.
          I was astounded he assumed
that he was living in a funny world—
a sense he did not learn from me
or even from his dad; no doubt
he had been born possessing it—
a gift that Nature in its laws
of continuity bestowed on him.
          And so, when perched upon
his high-chair throne, discarding food
this way and that as if there never
could be famine in the world,
feasting with the entire family,
his mom, his grandmother, his aunt,
the would-be chieftain of the clan
clapped his commanding hands

and beat them on the tray—applause
for me to imitate, and him to imitate
my imitation. This, too, appeared to him
hilarious, and every one of us
joined the hilarity; laughter, for sure,
had power to suffuse the universe.

       But after mom had put him into bed,
and sleep suspended laughter in the night,
his father told me of the operation
that he faced, his shoulder muscles had
to be tied up to hold the bones
within their sockets, and that meant
he'd have to change his occupation
as a landscaper; he'd have to start again
defining who at heart he was,
no longer keeper of the shrubs and trees,
stripped down to his identity
as husband and as father to a son.

      What laughter then could I
recover from such stunning news?
There was indeed a message
to be heeded from these facts: we all
must persevere no matter what
the obstacles; our love of children
must remain enough to keep us
doing what we have to do.
But is there laughter to be found
in grim necessity, in Nature howling out
what seems to us the logic of a whim?

      And thereby I proclaimed this to be so;
apostle of absurd defiance, I
crashed my fist down upon the wooden table
where we sat, and then my son,
in instantaneous response,
slammed his hand down so hard
he made the flaming candles
shudder in their wicks. We caught
the glitter in each other's eyes,

and in that moment we both realized
a revelation had occurred—a revelation
that released our laughter once again.
            We laughed beyond all reason
and beyond restraint, our uproar like
a banquet of the drunken gods,
our mad tears overwhelming us,
until our mutual cacophony
awoke the baby from protecting sleep
with cries confused and terrified.
            Confused myself, hopeful without
convincing evidence, I still
have one remaining blessing to bestow:
the wish that some unbidden day my grandson
will inherit laughter of another kind—
laughter most human in its sympathy—
to add to what already lies within
his muscles and his bones, when he,
whose voice contains wild mountain winds,
becomes his generation's caretaker,
the father of a father of a son.

LITERARY RAVENS

It was a sparkling Saturday in June—
A perfect day to drive an hour to town,
To browse the open marketplace,
Bump into chatty friends,
And purchase the fresh vegetables
Grown by our local farmers
And laid out in luminous display:
Lettuce and radishes, carrots,
Baby potatoes—white and red—
Scallions and spinach, testifying how
Amazing Mother Nature is
When She's in harmony
With cultivating human care.
      Returning home, we found the floor
Of our garage completely strewn
With bottles, cans, discarded paper,
Orange and banana peels.
I realized that I'd neglected
To roll down the rumbling door,
Thus leaving garbage pails
Exposed to swooping ravens
Who had emptied them. And here's
Where my adoring hymn to Nature,
My domestic saga of contentment,
Touches on what some of you,
Only the skeptical, incredibly
May find incredible.
      Corrected papers on the floor,
Included drafts of odes that I
Had recently composed about
These shining birds, praising
Their patience and persistence,
Their unusual intelligence,
Evoked their curiosity and, no doubt,
their vanity, as well, and tempted them

To read my rhapsodizing poems,
Translating them into their own
Raucous vernacular.
              They had, of course, admired them
And searched the teeming bounty
Of the tumbled garbage pails
For every luscious word
Their appetites could find therein.
I hope that you'll agree
No other explanation can account
For how the poems' revisions were
Deliberately arranged
Upon the telltale floor which otherwise
Would have to be explained merely
By chance or randomness.
              And in that glow of revelation I,
Enraptured and serene, considered how
Poetic art conjoined with Nature
Make a pair, as man and woman do,
Helpmates and complements,
And how, when merged with mind,
With soaring, speculating mind,
Inchoate Nature can reach out
In order to express Herself,
Thus giving substance to the very thought
Expressed, adding to what is real,
Transforming ordinary fact
Into the highest visionary form.
              My moment of transcendence passed—
Such moments, we all know, can't be
Sustained—and then my job was just
To tidy up the aggravating mess,
Restoring order to its mundane state.
My wife called out when I was done,
"Next time we go to town, make sure the door
Is closed so ravens can't get in."
I felt chagrined, I felt let down—

I kicked the damn offending door—
But wishing to assure her that
One mess like this was quite enough
To help complete a perfect day,
All I could think to say was "Nevermore."

IT'S MAY AGAIN

It's May again, and I'm still here to breathe
The wafted fragrance from the lilac bush
Because there's no work left for me to do,
My work is done; for better or for worse
I've finished what I would become, what I
Completed and have been, and so I'm free
To loiter in the fragrance of a lilac bush,
To feel the soothing sun as if its warmth
Were meant for consolation, meant for me.
The lilac bush, the streak of goldfinches
That glitter in their springtime hue—I'm here
To smell, to see strained laboring no more
to be already what I am,
No urgency except to pause and watch
Goldfinches in their golden fluttering.
I'm here, I still am here, with nowhere else
To long for or to go; and so I listen
To the booming of an early bee
As if he, too, is happy that it's May
Right here on earth, ready for what a bee
Needs to be ready for, and so I say
I'm ready to remain here longer in
The lilac air, to breathe the scented light
Of what remains of this remaining May.

OLD MAN WALKING

We could conceive that all the conditions for the first production of a living organism [existed] in some warm little pond . . . that a compound was chemically formed ready to undergo more complex changes.

—CHARLES DARWIN, *letter to Joseph Hooker, 1871*

It's balmy April and the maple buds,
All swollen red and now prepared to burst,
Beckon me forth to make my first spring hike
Across the field and down the woodland path
To sit beside the overflowing stream
And watch its eddies and its swirls, its crests
When leaping over stones, its spume and spray,
Its rainbow mist that arcs the scene.
        I'll sit on a smooth outcropping of rock,
Entranced by light reflected from wet stones,
Light shimmering where water undulates,
Staring at the stark spectacle without
Insignias or tokens of my friends
Who've died within the year; I will return
To see curled water swoop within itself,
To dwell upon the wafted splash of light,
Determined only to observe. Maybe
Old legs can't carry me so far this year;
Maybe I'll pack my lunch, but then turn back
Before I reach the stream if my hip won't
Obey my will's command; maybe for me
A final age of dwindling has begun,
And I'll return home with my blood subdued,
With disappointment shadowing my eyes
And only memory to serve as light,
My friends receding as I think of them,
Compelled to mull about our origins,
How water is our universal womb.
        My fear was accurate, although I tried
I couldn't make it to the chosen stream

And had to rest upon a rotting log before
I headed back, vowing to try again
In May or June, inspired, as Darwin was,
By "grandeur," nature's blind ability
To fabricate new complex forms, grandeur
Contending with profound dismay at nature's
Wastefulness—famine and violence,
An unrelenting process that began,
So awe-struck Darwin would surmise, merely
By random chance in some warm little pond
According to a shift in chemistry.
      Well, I'm not ready to give in to gloom;
Perhaps next month with the incentive that
The fullness of spring blooming brings—
Bounty exceeding ravenous decay—
I'll give my legs and hip another try
To hike me to the stream. I've gotten fond
By now of all my groping body parts,
Although no longer can I count on them
As once I could, just to enjoy, to be
Aware I am aware, to be in touch—
With what exactly I don't know, to watch
The spume play on the surging water that
Still seems to welcome the indifferent light.

MIDDAY MOTHS

I am high stepping through the rough tall grass
Sparkling with daisies in the uncut field;
Meandering, I brush a path to pass
Through constellations of white moths concealed

Within their shaded midday resting place
Until chance footsteps stirred them into flight.
They populate my planetary space
As if to rearrange the fractured light,

As if berserk with awe, as I am now
Just watching them, quite unprepared as they
To know how to respond, just watching how
We're all propelled in our own startled way.

So what shall I, enraptured, make of this—
This whirling plenitude of randomness?

THIS INSTANT NOW

Right here, this instant now,
watching a nameless stream
whose waters leap over protruding rocks
and then flow twisting forth
as if a message were inherent there
which careful watching somehow
might disclose, I see stark noonday sun
in its reflected light,
effulgent in its vanishing,
this instant here, this here right now.

Reflections on the water's flow
repeat a theme in which what is
right here, this instant now,
might well shine forth
at any place or any time, and has—
one day lost in a multitude of days—
according to an unconsoling law
my watching faithfully obeys.

A sudden surge of wind reveals
the image of my face right here
upon one rock above the water
as I watch, the foam my beard,
a crevice in the rock my down-turned mouth—
a face that vanished now
the blazing instant it appeared.

Nearing an end, my own,
among an endless multitude of ends
stretched back as far as I can see,
I am no closer to where comfort was
or is or might forever be,
unless I find it merely in the sight
of water washing over gleaming stones,

reflections on which I reflect
and thus contain somehow,
even as liquid light eludes my witnessing
right here this instant now, and now again,
and now and now and now and now.

THE WAR TO END ALL WARS

Despite the fact that I've lived long enough
to see the Cold War end, the Berlin wall
come crashing down, nuclear weapons
used only as a threat to counteract
a counter threat, I fear next century,
incredibly, may be less kind to all
of us as the scenario of fate
unfolds according to what nature is—
I mean our own, what humans are at heart.
        I still cringe when a noise resounds, even
an urgent human voice addressing me
from right behind my stiffened back, as if,
with fast reflexes I've inherited
from our long evolutionary past,
I'm able to avoid oncoming bombs.
There's nothing new in how I still react.
        My mother as a Russian child survived
pogroms and blasts from raids; she'd hide
inside a closet when a thunderstorm
occurred. For her, the basic difference
between blind Nature's random violence
in storms or floods, and human viciousness,
deliberate and willed, had been obscured.
But she could find no consolation or
no innocence in the apparent fact
that people, like the elements, do what
they are designed to do—to fight, to hurt,
according to our native genius in
contriving instruments that make us more
what we have always been. And yet we ask:
Is it too late to choose to change ourselves—
perhaps if we get desperate enough?
        We have survived so far, though not without
tremendous suffering, starvation we
have caused, forced marches in the gouging sun;
only two atom bombs have been deployed

in half a century of brutal strife
about just whom the one god really loves
and whom he therefore wants us to destroy.
It's true we haven't quite gone all the way
in letting roiling hate obliterate
our sympathies—at least not yet, although
we're almost there, almost at the sharp edge
where genius to destroy, the genius that
defines us most as if technology,
inherent in our genes, waiting its time,
has brought us to the brink where now we are.
        Who is this "us"? Whose panting faces do
I conjure up when hot revenge bristles
my startled hair and burns inside my heart?
Because I mourn my own mortality,
do I indeed want everyone to die?
If I cannot survive myself, do I
desire to have all humankind go down
into the stinking mud along with me?
Can that face be my face or are there others
hidden in the hills, or else behind
locked doors in alleyways of city slums
who wish extinction for my kind because—
because we don't believe what they believe.
        So here I am again distracted by
the ideologies that seem the cause of why
we hate and why we kill, prepared to fight
the final futile war, despite the fact
that everywhere on this tormented earth
mothers protect their children, fathers risk
themselves to aid their wives, their friends, sometimes
for strangers pleading by the road—as you
cry to me now or maybe I to you.

FROM
Laughter Before Sleep
(2011)

((

ONLY THE EVERGREEN

The only evergreen not always green,
With null November coming on,
The tamarack lets go its needles as I see
October flourish to its sullen end,
As if one season can encompass both
Mortality and immortality
In its unfolding golden blend.
Green needles brighten
In their languid mellowing:
Yellow turns gold, gold shades to bronze,
Repeated in the rippling lake,
So slowly over dwindling sunlit days
That I can comprehend transfigured trees
Are destined and designed
To go their modulating ways
To barrenness—and thus their going is
Contained within my mind.
The beauty of these evergreens
In their effulgent letting go,
Preparing for new beauty coming on—
The silence of bare branches
Underneath the silence of submerging snow—
Is such that I can almost let myself forget
How silence deepens to oblivion
Devoid of yellow, gold, or bronze,
Until all going finally is gone.

WOODPECKER REPRISE

Arriving from the prehistoric past,
out from the tangle of a dense pine grove,
its undulating flight of red dips and red glides
propels the pileated woodpecker
to the thick tamarack where I have nailed
a suet block for him to feast upon.

What a survival team we make
when we pair up our skills, though
his long ancestry has made it all these years
without my help! Still, something new
has come about as I exchange a meal for him
just for the opportunity to watch
the thrusting of his crested head,
in a red blur, into the suet block
that Mother Nature has contrived for him
with me as her convenient medium.

It seems she has decided that she wants
appreciation for her quirkiest designs—
improvisations and refinements that
inspire more variations still; she wants
approval for her handiwork, and who
can fault such motivation to invent?

That is where I come in: my consciousness
to praise, admire, and celebrate.
What else in all creation is so special
and unique, something not heretofore
existing in a mute, indifferent universe?
Observing him, I'm also the observer
of myself observing him—my own red passion in
my own reverberating light.

NAMING MOUNTAIN WILDFLOWERS

My guess is that they've blossomed here
for centuries. And there's forefather Adam,
whom I summon now in memory
to honor him because he was the first
to name the flowers and the animals!
Now with the help of books and friends,
I've learned what some are called,
so I elect to share the pleasure
of identifying them for others just
as I have learned their names, my friend, from you.

I'll start with showy Shooting stars
suggestive of the stars in the night sky—
and worthy to pledge faithfulness upon—
as if the heavens and the earth are one,
assuringly continuous
as propagating day, reposeful night,
connecting what appears to be apart.

Then I'll move on to Prairie Crocus
with its yellow center framed
by pallid purple petals tightly wound.
And since I'm thinking yellow-purple thoughts,
let me augment my growing list
with velvety Delphinium,
with trailing Clematis that binds itself
around unshapely fallen branches, logs,
as if, embraced, dead things
can cycle back to life and bloom
through the remembrance of inheritors.

Returning to the theme of yellowness
as in the Pasque flower in its purple frame,
I'll sound out Buttercup on my pursed lips
whose brilliant yellow can be found replete
amid the wooly, aromatic Sage.
And thus I have an image to describe
the concept of fecundity: Ah Buttercup,

my own cup runneth over with the names
of what I'm able to identify.
          In this beginner's list, my favorite
Is Old Man's Whiskers with its wispy look
of feathery long tufts, reminding me
of me! I am the rapt observer here,
alive this moment in cascading time,
author of the attachment that I feel
in naming their symmetric shapes—like Yellowbell
just listen hard and you can hear them ring),
and golden-centered Heart-Leaved Arnica,
and Glacier Lily, and tight Lupine buds
that will emerge as bluish-purple cones,
and pink to white to bluish Carpet Phlox;
and densely clustered Creeping Grape,
Wild Strawberry (not yet quite ripe enough
to feast upon), and Lemonweed
(which native women used in tea
to regulate when they gave birth),
prolific Balsamroot whose gaudy
yellow flowers amid gray-green leaves
display themselves as eager to be seen,
sticky Geranium, and Violets—
their blending shades and hues enlarge
a wanderer's most passionate imagining
of what his moment in the light allows.
          My cup—it runneth over with delight
as I walk on in wonder at my wondering,
and so I'll praise forefather Adam now
for his annunciations that first bonded him
to the lush. bounty of his fruitful world
and showed the rest of us the way,
and I'll give multiplying thanks
(accompanied by—listen!—colored bells)
to every fervent namer who devotedly

will follow me, as, Janet, I have followed you,
to celebrate a world of worded things,
the budding and unfolding of companionship
across all time and separating distances,
the vow of friendship that shared naming brings.

SONNETELLE OF THE DARK

I think the darkness changes at the end
With no light left to see the darkness swell—
Darkness that's neither enemy nor friend,
And nothing's left to question or to tell.

This undiscriminating dark without
Relief or variation or the choice
To protest or accept, believe or doubt,
Leaves only hissing silence with a voice.

There won't even be light enough to see
The temporary dark before a flash
Illuminates the branches of a tree—
The consolation of the thunder crash.

This dark knows nothing and it does not care;
This dark does not remember or pretend;
This dark is not aware it's not aware.
This is the changeless darkness at the end.

PARENTING PENGUINS

Since I was a small boy I've wanted to
raise penguins and to own a baby elephant.
Despite my Doctor Doolittle complex,
I knew I did not have the resources—
although our barn had space enough—
to be a mother elephant, but penguins, yes,
that did seem possible to me
throughout my adolescent years
and even into marriage when we had
three human children of our own.

But when in fleeting time the kids grew up
and left us in the house alone
to live their independent lives,
the thought of penguins popped back
in my mind and seemed to nestle there.
Why not? It's not impossible—what else
would be such fun to do—to romp
with penguins in the lonely afternoons?
Especially I liked the thought
it was the father penguin who
sat on the egg and incubated it,
keeping it safe from harm, keeping it warm
while resting on its father's feet
beneath a special flap of skin.

I wrote to tell my son about
the plans I was considering,
but he assumed some gentle teasing
would be his appropriate response,
and so he did some research on the needs
of penguins under human care.

Since they are social animals,
he tactfully replied, the minimum
I'd have to take into my care was ten,
and twenty would be better still;
I'd have to build a pool that was
at least fifteen feet at the deepest end;

supplying fish for them would cost me
several thousand bucks a year;
and, finally, the crushing detail that
weakened my resolution to proceed:
someone would have to be assigned to feed
the penguins six or seven times a day.
          "No way will I feed twenty penguins
seven times a day!" my wife proclaimed.
"We have six cats and that's enough;
including you, that's seven mouths to feed."
But on our anniversary my wife
presented me with twenty penguins
and an elephant, their bellies plump with cotton,
all approving me with rolling eyes.
          And so that ended it, and so
I wrote back to my expert son—
expositor of penguin happiness—
to thank him for the research he had done.
No further fantasy of parenting
to build on there. I can't erase
from my adjusted mind
the picture of tame penguins frolicking,
but I've concluded, even though
our children are dispersed across the continent,
I'd better stick to human fathering.

JASPER

        Concealed in the lush flower garden as
an evening storm comes on, hunting perhaps
or only passing time, Jasper, so I assume,
is thinking thoughts that cautious cats
have immemorially thought.
        My wife, preparing soup, steps out
the kitchen door to summon him;
uncertain for an instant, Jasper
considers if it is beneath
his dignity to come when called.
        He pauses at her feet, goes limp, so she
can lift him up and bring him in the house.
"Good Jasper boy," she says, and I assume
he understands. But she's not finished
with her accolades: "Handsome fellow,
your ancestors were surely kings,"
augments her praise, which he acknowledges
by leaping on the counter for his meal,
then, satisfied, he settles in a chair,
his favorite, dreaming no doubt what cats
have immemorially dreamed.
        And I can only guess what thoughts
float through my wife's reclusive mind
as she returns to slicing celery and carrots
for her secret recipe. "More pepper"
might be all the conscious words she needs,
though maybe some uncertain thoughts
with no connection to preparing soup—
thoughts of our distant daughter's
inconclusive diagnoses—darkens
an underlying mood, a shadow mood
of which perhaps she dimly is aware.
        All this, of course, is just my guess
which may have no relationship to her,
revealing only something about me,
and yet what might connect observing
Jasper emerging from his hiding place,

and what I think my wife might possibly
be thinking now, is galaxies beyond
what reasoned words can comprehend.
        Jasper wakes up and looks at me;
I think he thinks there may be something
on my mind that might pertain to him;
his body stiffens as he fixes on
some rustling sound outside the door.
I tell my wife, "A cat will bristle
at the slightest shift of wind," but she replies that
"Something recently has worried him;
perhaps he picks the worry up from you."
        Can that be true? Can she intuit
something about me by watching Jasper
scamper from his chair? Or am I able
to detect what might be troubling her
by what she seems to have observed
in how Jasper and I respond to what
each thinks is on the other's mind?
Perhaps the singular connection here
is that we hear the same wind at the door
or else the barking of our neighbor's dogs
whom Jasper, a survivor, outmaneuvers
with his many lives—a Jewish cat,
so let his enemies take note!
        My wife adds pepper to the soup—
a careful sprinkle, nothing more, tastes it
and, yes, she's satisfied, as I will be
come dinnertime, and Jasper, sleeping
in the chair that recollects his shape,
is satisfied, and everywhere on earth
each household cat, survivors all,
content in its own mystery, gives aid
and consolation to the wives and husbands
who depend on them to fill the silences
where words can't reach, to fill them,
and, beyond uncertainties, be satisfied.

AN ELEPHANT BY ARISTOTLE

      Elephants also need to dream,
And when one suffers from insomnia,
So Aristotle wrote in his vast work,
"On Animals," painstakingly described,
The cure that will restore him to good health
Can be effected if his shoulders are
"rubbed with warm water, olive oil, and salt."
In his discerning study of the animals,
Amphibians and fish, insects and birds,
Describing how their organs serve their needs,
He claimed the legendary elephant
Exceeded other creatures with "its wit
And its intelligence;' though what he meant
By wit is open to our speculation still.
      I recently had graduated from
An elite college where I learned all this
And much more that I didn't know—
Delightful as such knowledge was—
How to apply it to my life. Depressed,
I was uncertain whether I should be
A doctor or a lawyer or just make
A lot of money as my uncle had.
      My roommate's family lived on a farm;
They had an empty barn with stalls
That weren't being used. And so I thought,
Before I could collect myself and make
The consequential choice of a career,
I would, still single, unattached,
Indulge myself and thus acquire
A baby elephant, since Aristotle had
Assured me "They are easy tempered and
Domesticated easily."
My plan was that I'd keep him in the barn
All languid summer long, and in the fall
I'd sell him to the zoo up in the Bronx
With an agreement that I'd have

The right to visit him at leisure on
Slow weekends and on holidays.
     I need to warn you that this favorite
Remembrance only has begun: unlikely
As it sounds, an ad from Bloomingdales
Appeared in the bland New York Times
Announcing that they'd purchased, and would give
To some deserving zoo, a baby elephant
Whose mother had been shot and killed—
No doubt by hunters poaching ivory—
Just like the elephant of my imagining,
The one I'd always wanted to adopt.
     You need to know we get names wrong
In our dyslexic family, and I called Macy's
By mistake, but when they transferred me
To an impatient salesman in
Their stocked department of stuffed toys,
I realized my error and hung up the phone.
And when I next called Bloomingdales,
The manager enquired what zoo
I represented and expressed contempt
When I explained quite simply that
My motive was my love of elephants:
Was that too hard for him to understand?
     I had to borrow money, piles of it,
To cover the outrageous asking price,
From my bemused and wealthy uncle with
A bachelor's flair for wild extravagance,
And I was able, you'll be pleased to know,
To outbid the astounded New York zoos
With their tight budgets and constraints.
     All summer long my elephant and I
Cavorted in the purple clover field
Or splashed each other in the lily pond;
Ears still, he'd sneak up from behind
And put his trunk between my legs,
Lift up, and tumble me head forward
In the cart wheel spin I had to learn

To play my part in our invented game.
This well might be considered wit, "panting
A sound just like a sighing man," as Aristotle
Had foreseen so many books ago.

      So, Aristotle, thanks to you I knew
Just how to rub the shoulders of
My parabolic pachyderm
With the prescribed ingredients
To spare him from such dreams as cause
Insomnia, dread falling dreams of loneliness,
Bereavement, or abandonment.

      My laughing gratitude calls out to you,
Dear founding father of philosophy,
Observer with an eye for wonder and
Astonishment, for how detail and fact
And information, tempered with, ah yes!
A touch of delicate embellishment,
Can be recalled to rescue us from gloom
And flourish forth some waking happiness.

GENIE

A long-time pessimist, having observed
first-hand the vanity of human
aspirations and desires, Rabbi Ezekiel,
now old and burdened with regrets,
"a daughter married to a lazy schlub,
a son in faraway America,"
surveyed the Mediterranean shore
of ancient embarkations and retreats.
Searching the beach for spiraled shells
as fragile souvenirs of transient life,
he stubbed his toe on a blue bottle
almost hidden underneath the sand.

He brushed the grit off of its sides,
and LO! out popped a genie with white curls,
a shiny yarmulke upon his head.
"Don't stare at me like that!" the genie
reprimanded him, "why shouldn't Jews
have Jewish genies to attend their needs?"

"It's usual to get three wishes,"
he declared, "according to the formula,
but you're not looking at a genie of
high rank; all I can offer you is just
one wish, so make your choice judiciously."

A pious thought occurred to glum Ezekiel—
that he might make a wish to ease
the struggle underneath our common sun
of animals and humans, all alike
in needing food and being doomed to die.
Surely the genie would approve
this altruistic sentiment. "I'll wish,"
he murmured, "for a universal peace
to end all forms of prejudice."

The genie slapped his head, knocking
his yarmulke askew. "Oy veh!" he cried,
"that isn't possible. By nature Nature

preys upon itself; after the flood
Yahweh revised the rules so Noah could
devour red meat as well as plants,
despite the dread that caused the animals—
see chapter nine of Genesis.
You'll have to improvise another wish."

    Ezekiel thought hard and the idea
leapt to his mind that if he can't assuage
some suffering afflicting humankind,
maybe he still might aid his fellow Jews.
And so he wished that oil be found right there
on that stark shore where they now stood—
oil would help Israel's economy.
"That's a humungous wish for me to grant—
a worn-out genie who is making do
with worn-out powers. Try again,
but stick to something personal
like winning the town lottery, or else
relief for that arthritis in your back.
Don't keep your private feelings bottled up,"
the genie added, pleased with his own quip.

    "I must confess," Ezekiel replied.
"I've been denied much pleasure in my life,
serving my congregation, following
the strictures of our holy book.
Here is a recent photo of my wife—
she ain't what you'd call beautiful.
Can't you improve her looks a little bit,
make her a little thinner, sexier,
to warm the chill of my declining age?"

    The genie stared at the creased picture of
the rabbi's wife: after a pause—drawn out
and hanging heavy in the air—he said,
"Let's see if oil can be discovered here;
for sure, we'll have to count on lady luck."

    A month goes by, and once again
Ezekiel is wandering along
the hieroglyphic beach, observing foam

that bubbles its insistent syllables,
and it amuses him to conjure up
a scene in which his genie finds a bottle
almost buried in the sand, rubs it, and LO!
another genie pops out with a flourish
of his velvet shawl. The rabbi likes
the logic that wish-granting genies must
depend on other genies who can grant
their wishes if acknowledged as their own.
        And with this floating fantasy in mind—
of genies bringing forth more genies
multiplying on into infinity—
Ezekiel knows that though he'd like to be
a high-ranked genie with the power to
alleviate the sorrows of the world,
at least those sorrows caused by us,
by granting wishes that reside within
the rounded realm of possibility,
he'll have to be content at last just telling
genie jokes to strangers, making friends
whose laughter frolics in the lilting foam.

FROM
To Love That Well
(2013)

❨

THERE'S STILL TIME LEFT

I must confess I'm really proud
of certain genes of mine,
though surely not unique,
that I would like to see passed on
and thrive across the generation gaps
and on into a future well beyond
what I'm now able to conceive.
　　My opera-hungry gene
scaling the heights of ecstasy—
the passions of an aching
or a joyous heart;
the gene that takes inordinate delight
in Jewish jokes, their fantasies
of triumph over awesome odds;
the gene that cherishes
the life-affirming animals
and can imagine raising baby bears
or elephants, in my back yard
as if the whole lush world
were a safe home protected
by a caregiver, a nurturer,
a universal father-mom like me.
　　And so I bid my best
most celebrating genes go forth
in spite of prejudice,
in spite of hatreds inexplicable
(the cutthroat stalks the unlit streets,
terrorists eye the marketplace)
to spread their daffy cheerfulness
and do their double-helix dance as if
there's music and there's laughter
stirring in their genesis.
　　Yes, I am optimistic since
my five-year-old precocious grandson
loves Sergei Prokofiev:
the duck, the cat, the little bird,

each with its own melody,
the hunters and the grandfather
depicted by the bounce of a bassoon—
so let all preying wolves take note.
It's not too late to set things right,
subdue the drive to dominate,
subdue the instinct to assert
dominion over other lives
with their own eccentricities.
        O accidental genes—random,
fortuitous, and yet my own,
uncertain of your usefulness,
genes searching to find out your way,
transcending greed, transcending hate,
I must believe there's still time left;
it's not too late! it's not too late!

WHEAT FIELD WITH CROWS

That rough path plunging deep
into the tangle of the golden field
seems to allow no turning back
once one has entered in.
Has my life taken me this far?

I watch the flow of fleeting wings,
receding over grain unharvested,
toward dark blue sky that's shading into
darker blue then deeper into black:
are death and ripeness inextricable?

Those agitated wings, are they
just fragments of a larger dark,
expanded and expanding far beyond
the road, the field, the vague horizon's edge,
beyond my sight, beyond imagining?

RETELLING

Born in New York in 1929,
I'm just past eighty-two years old. My mother,
nurturer and worrier supreme,
arrived from Russia with her family
when she was only two in order to
escape the persecutions there, which she,
of course, could not recall, and so she took
her older sister's memories as if
they truly were her own—the horseback Cossacks
crashing madly down the hills with rape
and burning in their eyes—and now, retold
and kept alive, these memories are mine.
        My father was a New Deal senator
for whom the Great Depression carried fear
of deprivation and stark poverty
that was a burden all his striving days.
His widowed mother came from Germany,
I don't know why, so much remains unknown,
but World War II taught me that Nazis were
evil and we Americans were good;
such clarity was comforting, but right
and wrong, the sanctioning of violence,
have fallen to confusion and dispute,
though I knew well, and surely do so still,
the Holocaust tells us we can't rely
on human mercy, pity, or constraint,
or any God justice might comprehend.
        My father died at forty-six after
five strokes, and his three brothers likewise died
in middle age. I am astounded I
have managed to hang on so long even
with help from my iambic pace-maker,
my time-keeper for keeping time, although
I think hearty determination plays
a vital part that can affect brute facts
of DNA and one's inheritance.
        Mourning consumed my sister's wedding vows,

her search for simple trust; the dread
she'd be again abandoned by a man—
if not by death, then by inconstancy—
has proven true, though it has toughened her;
she's independent as a lioness.
        And so I've learned endurance matters most:
one soft midsummer afternoon I swam
across a lake's reflected light; I paused
on the far shore to eat a tangerine—
a lunch-box gift from an admiring kid—
then stroke by rhythmic stroke, I swam back where
I started from in harmony so sweet
it seemed contentment had suffused the air.
        My early marriage failed: no doubt I was
too needful for a compensating son
to fill the emptiness my father left;
no longer did his voice inform the wind.
Yet my best high school buddies have remained
in faithful touch, despite griefs of their own:
friendship assuaging loneliness was mine,
and mine the comfort of round bales of hay
in fields reposing in the harvest sun
whose vistas steadied me in my own place.
        I have been married fifty years this time:
I wonder where the whirling years have gone,
like mist blown through a valley passageway,
though we have built log houses, grown
begonias and abundant vegetables,
planted two rows of hardy apple trees,
and made a home for turtles, dogs, and cats.
        Also, we've raised three kids: a carpenter
perfectionist, a green-thumbed landscaper,
and, to our inexplicable surprise,
a daughter famous as a rock-climber
despite the fact—proving that genes do not
control the crucial choices one does make—
my down-to-earth wife is afraid of heights.
Only our youngest son is married and
he lives across the ocean in Kauai

with our solitary grandchild whom
we cannot read to when he goes to bed.
        But I am gratified by having taught
for almost sixty years (my goal)—a record
for commitment I can boast about: I am
the Cal Ripkin of academia.
And I've enjoyed preparing for each class;
all-caring Shakespeare shaped my consciousness
and deepened me with probing inwardness.
"I've meant for some time now to thank you for
your Shakespeare class," one student, ten years
afterwards, wrote in a time-transcending note.
        I strain to make my poems appear complete,
and yet I've published eighteen books, inspired
by my invented brother, my indulgent,
pun-addicted, taunting twin, his packed
heart fortified with words, whose gambler's zest
for taking chances and for doubling down,
for wooing damsels unavailable,
expanded my vain, pungent appetites.
Walking a log across a waterfall
one foggy afternoon, he tumbled on
a jutting stone and broke his neck; yet I
restored him back to life in my next book,
bemused by his instructive punishment.
        Such poems were meant to make him laugh—like one
in which I'm turned into a mother duck
by evolution's random quackery
when an abandoned cracked egg hatched under
my probing fingertip so that the duckling
followed after me as if somehow,
even in this indifferent universe,
fortuitous protection may be found.
        Some poems have rhymes, some round refrains, to add
to fertile nature's symmetries—pinecones,
snowflakes, the wings of butterflies-although
it's much to hope for that my poems, aspiring
to survive the tree-uprooting storms,

will long outlive my body's being here.
      Maybe actual books—their touch, their smell—
will soon be obsolete, forgotten with
so many cherished things: the operas
of Mozart with their universal themes
of lust and undeserved forgiving love,
melodically lush in airy forms,
that soar beyond causality and stun
the contrite sinner with astonishment
like matter, space, and time—physical laws
emerging from pure, primal nothingness.
      I'm not sure such a brief account should sketch
this early memory (I might have been
just three) because it's possible 1 have
contrived it from a wish for permanence
eternally composing Mom and Dad
who hold hands underneath a willow tree,
the dangling branches half obscuring them,
their gazes dappled in the evening glow.
      Perhaps I've seen a picture in a book
with a log house beneath a purple cloud
that looks like home as it's about to rain
and sleek crows huddle on the slanted roof.
One can't be certain going back so far
what has been fantasized and what is real,
although the picture feels as if it's true.
      With all our children tangled in their lives,
my wife and I reside here in the woods
with a vast panoramic view across
the Mission mountain range whose jagged peaks
hold timeless snow throughout the summer months;
hawks circle overhead and then streak off and leave me to
imagine where they weave
their perishable nests, sufficient for
the season of their need, and pass the night
as when I pull the covers up and let
the tell-tale images come as they will:
uncertain faces looming in the mist.

THE RAINBOW AND THE OWL

The time allotted me to spend on earth
has been almost already spent,
and still the world is cursed with suffering—
starvation glaring in the children's eyes.
Other than loyalty to friends,
I do not know what else I might have done
to sweeten human fellowship, relieve
those destined to their solitude, and so
I won't be able to depart in peace.
　　　Perhaps it is presumptuous to think
I might have shown more kindness, more
compassion to the needy and the weak,
and to the ever-present poor
more generosity, yet what
alternative in summing up my life
does aged imagination still find plausible?
Serenity requires that I believe
some work I've done, some lovely, liquid, soothing
utterance, should have an influence
that lasts beyond impersonal decay.
　　　I wonder if a summoned memory
might yet be able to assuage remorse,
maybe an image of the spinning world
like sitting by a waterfall, whose spume
reflects a rainbow's arc, waiting
for someone to arrive to rescue me
from living merely my own life—someone
whose yearnings I can recognize; or like
a white owl in a hemlock tree, as if
illuminated from within, who sits
hunched in his hushed awareness of roused wind,
knowing no more than he has need to know—
his future indistinguishable from
the curved grip of his talon-haunted past.

But there is not sufficient consolation
even in rapt contemplation of
astounding nature's vast variety,
its beetles and its spiders and its ants,
as if intended just to flourish as display;
I fear imperfect solace must suffice.

His great wings spread, the silent owl,
with golden eyes, swoops down to snatch
a vole he hears a foot beneath the snow,
seeking the safety of his tunneled nest,
whose one-year life is thus cut short.

And *oh!* I see a million hands reach out
to everyone who aches with hunger or
whose body is clenched in with dread,
to every cringing creature on the globe
of my imagining; I'm suddenly
aware that what enlarges me is not
alone the gathered story of my life;
though inconclusive as a rainbow in
the spread spume of a steady waterfall,
a surge of sympathy, impersonal,
and yet my own, appears embodied by
uprisen, swirling wind that warps
a white owl's shadow streaking on
the silver surface of sleek moonlit snow.

A GHOST IN WINTER

A misty ghost, with features
I could not identify; appeared
as I was walking home at dinner time;
although his arms reached out,
he had no words to offer me.
Slick icicles were melting from
the neon signs along the avenue,
and I paused momentarily to wonder if
the ice floes at the northern pole,
were breaking up and changing course
as billions of receding galaxies
are hurtling outward toward
no destination I might call my own.
I asked the shimmer of a ghost,
its breath no different than the breath
of an exhausted polar bear
waiting in vain beside a water hole
for an unwary seal to appear,
to tell me if he'd help identify
some personal and singular regret
not yet unacknowledged in my effort
to confront the silent void
with just the dignity of truthfulness.
If only I'd embraced the shadow
of the past, learned ancient Greek
so I could read Homer's *Iliad*,
the blind bard's weeping epic of
grief inescapable for all of us
desire-tormented creatures—what
we've always been, and are,
and yet to hear the soothing flow
of his unhesitating voice that sings
above the dark temptation of the sea,
of sunlight glinting on a graven shield.

Such incantation might make possible
acceptance of the unacceptable;
Homer's enduring art might yet
enable me to hold myself unshaken by
the vision of our universe
accelerating toward oblivion,
and contemplate without a shudder
planetary variation here.
        A shapeless haze of breath,
pulsing in neon red, leapt forth
from that unspeaking faceless ghost
who disappeared among
the swirling multitude departing there,
thus leaving me abandoned
with an evanescent thought
I hardly recognized as mine:
I will not be alive to save
the unsuspecting polar bear.

GALACTIC MOTH WITH EYESPOTS

Not just our Milky Way, nor just Andromeda
for company, but, as we've learned,
billions of galaxies spin out
beyond what we'd imagined as beyond,
with space expanded by dark energy
we can't explain—like consciousness
confounded by awareness of itself.
     And in each galaxy billions of stars
await perhaps to be observed
as if some purpose in their being watched
spontaneously might emerge.
Cosmic debris blasts streaming by
or gathers into super-heated dust
to give birth to another galaxy.
The stars outnumber grains of sand
on all the shores and deserts of our earth
whose end is fated when the sun shall burst
in a spectacular display
with no one left alive for wonderment.
     Some thoughts remain unthinkable,
yet I can comprehend the paradox
my mind contains the knowledge that
it cannot know itself—and presto! my
own bafflement brings blazing forth
the singular stupendous insight
of my stupefying insignificance,
my momentary place as awed beholder of
red-shifted and receding galaxies.
     But here I am in the familiar landscape
I call home with objects I can touch,
the smooth rail of my cedar deck
that looks out on a snow-capped, mountain range;
I'm here with things whose names I know

that I can utter to the wind—
names that distinguish nuthatches from
flitting chickadees; I stroll beside
the birch I planted twenty years ago
now turning yellow in October light.
        And now I pause to scrutinize
one shaking leaf supporting a brown moth,
with eyespots circled on its wings
designed to scare off predators,
his delicate antennae seeking
consolation from autumnal warmth.
He braves the waning season as
I cheer him on, stupendous for just being
what he is in his green birch-leaf world,
triumphant for another shining day,
perhaps exhausted or fulfilled,
silently holding on there to survive.

for the lives I won't have time to live;
I'm green, *oh green-o,* in the melodies
I hum beneath the intake of my breath,
and when I contemplate the purple depths
of darkened sky with clouds outlining
migratory birds, I know at night
my heart will still be green, the green of emerald,
in the fine shimmer of its crystal light.

EMERALD

       Unbidden, a green memory
sprang forth, so overwhelming
in its clarity, it leapt across
three quarters of a century:
I stood before a countertop
of jewelry, eye height, beside
my father who had brought me to
that "five and dime" store in the Bronx
       Among the many rings displayed,
one gleaming emerald shore there
surpassing all the rest, and, firmly set
within a silver band, it was on sale
just for one dollar that my father
told the saleslady I'd saved.
       I bought the ring to give my mother
on their wedding anniversary;
I can still see her squeeze it on,
stretch her thin fingers out
that glowing morning to display
how perfectly it fit. I marveled
at the smoothness of her hands.
       I live now on a mountain-side,
the northern country of the evergreens—
spruce, cedar, ponderosa pines,
tall tamaracks reflecting in a lake
that quivers green and greener as
rough wind withdraws into the forest shade.
       From my high room I look out far
at darkened green of winter firs
whose branches are bent down with snow;
and I can see pale green in springtime when
the softer tips of boughs extend new growth;
even dense shadows as the sun descends
seem tinted with a greenish hue.
Despite accumulated years, I'm green
with inexperience; I'm green with envy

From
Clayfeld Holds On
(2015)

☾

BOB PACK'S INVOCATION TO CLAYFELD

By listening to what you say about
ephemerality and love,
I memorize your memories of what
in fact occurred, but also I'm enhanced
by your far-ranging fantasies, which have
a substance of their own and thus
possess the power to affect my life.
　　　The pleasure that you take adds to my own
when you evoke the twistings of desire,
a sheep clothed in the body of a wolf,
through innuendoes and equivocations,
not to be evasive, only to be
accurate about uncertainty
of motivation and intent—
as when a photon beam is flashed
through two small slits in an obstructing wall
behind which a reflecting screen displays
what the experimenter sees: the pattern
of a wave or else a particle,
with double meanings like a pun.
Might not that unpredictability
apply to you and me—each one of us
the other's plausible alternative,
although each double thought remains
a rumination of my own?
　　　The waterfall you hiked to in your youth
exists without someone's observing it,
but the pale girl who walked with you
through brambles up the mountainside,
who shared your rapture as the spume
composed a rainbow of its own, she might
be a composite of some other girls
you loved—or maybe you invented her
out of a wish, a dream, a reverie.

I need your fantasies so I
can witness my own life as if
it were a story in a gilded book,
replete with sorrows, disappointments,
foolishness, but still a comedy
affirming laughter aged perspective brings
of how lust lights the way to love.
          Ah! love, redeeming love, although
at bottom bodily, first sexual,
yet reaching out to humankind—
such love sought always to emerge in you
as if "Be fruitful, multiply!"
was a commandment to conceive
your self-proliferating self anew.
          Clayfeld, my doppelganger, as I'm yours—
quadruple if you count the two of us
as one—go forth with widened eyes
among proliferating bear grass like
a constellation in the spangled woods,
and journey where your heart revives
the need to reinvent yourself.
          The waterfall, composed of molecules,
quarks indivisible, is also
an epiphany incarnate
in the airy ambience of words evoking
your own covenant with Nature,
represented as a girl reposing on
a lichen-softened ledge, her forehead gleaming
with the waterfall's transparent spray—
a girl whose name you might remember
and hold dear. Perhaps you can recall
the shimmer of her hair, her heated cheeks,
the leaf-entangled light that glistened
on her shoulders as you kissed her
and, without constraint, she put her arms around
your neck, returning your uncertain kiss.
          And so your memory, though improvised,
completes what might have been, and so

the past can be doubly restored
by apprehending my own finite self,
aware of its own finitude, aware
of its compelling need for company.
       Dear Clayfeld, variant of who I am
in this observer-fabricated universe,
watch over me, attend me now,
and let the waterfall appear
unchanging in its changeability,
its little rainbow lifted in its spray,
and cherished simply for its flowing here.

A BLUE HERON APPEARS TO CLAYFELD

Meandering along the riverbank,
accompanied by his like-minded friend,
Clayfeld observes a blue-gray heron
with its neck curled back, its long thin legs
stretched out behind the whir of wings,
streak right above the roiling river's flow.
But Clayfeld wants to offer more
than wordless awe as his response;
he wishes to participate somehow
in that surprising spectacle,
to pluck from unresponsive silence
a fine shimmering analogy
to share with his uplifted friend.
        Clayfeld wants his enjoyment of
the rhythm of the heron's giant wings,
the river undulating under him,
to amplify what he and his tall friend
had witnessed just a flash ago.
        But nothing comes to mind, the shock of blue
resists comparison as if the bird
must not be seen as more than its own self,
as if Clayfeld's observing him
contributes nothing to the scene—and yet
Clayfeld's perceived irrelevance invites
acknowledgement which somehow then provides
a misty aura for the spectacle.
        Extemporizing to his friend,
as he is wont to do, Clayfeld would thus
include himself as part of the event,
and he reiterates the whir and streak
of unanticipated white and blue,
the plumed black line above the heron's eye,
the dagger glint of its extended bill.

So Clayfeld's voice ascends above
his normal baritone as he declaims
that his awareness of the heron's
separate, unique identity
released in him a surge of pleasure
instantaneous as the blue heron's
passing over undulating water with
its ice floes glowing in the mid-day sun.
        And Clayfeld's lanky friend lifts up
tip-toe to his exalted height,
flapping his long arms like a heron's wings,
revealing that he might have been
a heron in a prior life, cascading over
this same river in the hurtling wind;
and maybe Clayfeld was a heron too—
why not? they share a common heritage,
his friend proclaims, a common fate.
        A grayish blur of blue, the heron
disappears around the river bend,
and Clayfeld's improvising friend,
his outstretched arms still wavering,
glides down within himself and settles
smoothly on the stony shore
before astonished Clayfeld's gaze; and there,
poised in the winter sun, he shines forth
permanent and palpable in actual
friendship's legendary light
with his imaginary folded wings.

CONFRONTING CLAYFELD

Pausing for breath on a large fallen tree,
Clayfeld must have been watching longer
than he realized, for now declining light
upon the snow-bedazzled mountaintop
reveals blue shades and purple shadows
down its crevices that guide his view
to where the thrusting tree line ends,
the swaying tips of evergreens.
And Clayfeld wonders if his sense
of this illuminated mountain's vast
impersonality can free him now
from being only who he is.
A measure of detachment from
his personal desires has broadened,
he believes, his own capacity
to care for animals and friends,
so that the very act of taking care
becomes for him its own reward.
How fortunate, he thinks, confronting his
deep longing to transcend himself, that he
is able to conceive of selflessness—
a thought which seems to come from somewhere
far beyond his own volition or his will
and takes the form of serendipity.
The very concept of a selfless self
is like a happening without a cause
which then inspires happiness,
though Clayfeld knows that happiness
remains contingent and ephemeral.
Yet Clayfeld chooses still to focus
on the paradox that he feels most himself
when he regards his life as if he might
have read it in a book—a life about
a lover waiting by a waterfall,
a credible alternative to what
he can remember of himself.

And, suddenly, out from the underbrush,
a startled moose emerges with its antlers
gleaming in a splotch of sun, its spittle
sparkling in its beard, smelling of urine
to attract a mate; his presence is
so overwhelming that shocked Clayfeld,
apprehending him, is shaken from his trance,
back to his solitary self.
            He tastes his acid fear within his lungs
as its gigantic head, with flattened ears,
sways back and forth, about to charge
and trample him into the silent ground.
Clayfeld is flushed with the sensation of
his body's readiness to run or hide
behind a boulder or a hemlock tree
in caring for his one, his only life.
            And yet in Clayfeld's overheated mind–
his mind reduced to his own dread—
he knows he is preparing to relate
his threatening encounter
with a stamping, wide-eyed moose
to a trustworthy friend—someone,
perhaps, who wonders why this story of
personal fear must mean so much to him.

CLAYFELD'S REVERSAL

Clayfeld goes to the hospital to have his
pacemaker checked out.
To his surprise, his heartbeat has become
more regular. His doctor can't make sense
of such unprecedented change, and orders
that more diagnostic tests be done.
The tests show would-be poet Clayfeld's heart
has gone back to a normal beat,
that his condition actually has been
restored to what it used to be
so many unrecorded years ago.
"It is as if you have regained your youth,"
Clayfeld's astonished doctor says.
"My heart beats on iambically again—
yes, iamb that iamb defines me best,"
prosodic Clayfeld quips; "no longer
can my friends call me an anapest."
"Go home and tell your wife the news,"
his flustered doctor urgently replies.
The drive home through a mountain pass,
with Mozart streaming from the radio,
leads into vistas of a gleaming lake
with a swift waterfall cascading down
a distant outcropping of rocks,
creating its own spume and mist
where afternoon reflected light
composes a twin rainbow of
surpassing clarity. Elated Clayfeld
wonders what his wife will make
of this reversal, his regaining youth.
"What if she's frightened and can't follow me
in such a turnabout?" gasps Clayfeld
out loud to himself, his spirits dwindling in
the depths of thought. What if she feels rejected
by a restoration she can't share—
as if I have abandoned her to face
declining age all by herself?

Holding the wheel with his left hand, Clayfeld
places his right hand on his heart to see
if his grim apprehension of his wife,
stunned and recoiling from his news,
has shocked his pulsing heartbeat back
into irregularity again,
and, almost swerving off the road,
Clayfeld recalls how he first met his wife
skiing in Montreal: she was about
to plunge down the steep undulating slope,
her cheeks as red as her red hat,
flushed by a rushing surge of rousing wind.
        Yet maybe they first met in Florida
with her emerging from the sea,
her body glistening in the gold glare
of unobstructed midday sun.
What made these scenes converge within his mind?
confabulating Clayfeld asks himself;
what law of complementing opposites?
        When he arrives at home, Clayfeld discerns
something indeed is wrong. His wife looks pale
and her lips tremble as she speaks:
"1 think that you've grown tired of our life,"
she says. "I think you think that you might need
something quite new, perhaps a change of heart,
to keep your so-called spirits up."
That instant, call it fate, or call it
serendipity, the flashing phone chimes out
a prerecorded Mozart melody.
A message from the hospital proclaims
that Clayfeld's tests had been misread:
his offbeat heart remains unchanged.
In a lunge, in a bump, in a bounce, in a leap,
his heart skips to its old, familiar,
anapestic beat—as when a man of grief
in a wild whirling swoon, a vertigo,
falls uncontrollably in love.
And Clayfeld feels miraculous relief.

STAR-CROSSED CLAYFELD

  Clayfeld enjoys identifying stars,
seeing the constellations as old myths
described them—like the warrior Orion
or like Capricorn the fish-tailed goat.
Clayfeld imagines he's descended from
some hardy ancient seafarer
who braved the monsters of the deep
and navigated by familiar stars
in search of some exotic land, perhaps
an island filled with holy ornaments.
  Yet Clayfeld also is well read
in modern science, big bang theory,
quantum randomness, chaos complexity,
and so he knows that space and time
came into being out of nothingness
when the exploding bang occurred.
"Incredible!" astonished Clayfeld
muses to himself while wondering
if human creativity also
emerges out of nothingness, and if
all matter, everything that is,
is fated to be swallowed up
by primal nothingness again.
  Clayfeld conjectures whether the fixed laws
of mathematics—everywhere the same
throughout the universe—existed
previous to when the bang occurred,
despite the paradox that there
was absolutely nothing in the void
before conceivable space / time began.
  His meditations cause his vertigo,
though there is something quite exalting
in his dizziness—as if the human mind
deliberately was designed
for wonder and dumbfounded awe.

        Clayfeld, however, looks up at the stars
simply because he likes the show of lights—
no complicated motive there—
and it amused him to speculate
some star-struck sailor might have been
reminded by one faint configuration of
his own protective father's goat.
Despite this pleasing possibility,
the thoughts of nothingness will not release
its unrelenting hold on Clayfeld's mind.
    He tries to concentrate and once again
he fixes on the spectacle of stars:
the night sky never seemed more luminous,
a swooping meteor more radiant—as if
some meaning were about to be revealed
to free him from lifelong uncertainty.
But in that instant Clayfeld's elevated mood
collapses in despondency without
an explanation he can specify.
    Yet there is great Orion holding out
his shield against Taurus the mighty bull
about to charge with his great gleaming horns;
and there is Capricorn the goat
that suckled infant Zeus when he
was threatened by demented Chronus who,
if not prevented, would devour his son—
a goat much like the one Clayfeld had raised
when just a boy on his grandfather's farm.

FROM
All One Breath
(2019)

☾

SNOW GEESE RETURNING

Standing on the shore of Freezeout Lake
This March here in Montana I observe
Snow geese migrating back to Canada
Where they will court and mate and feed

Upon succulent weeds. And I can see
A coasting row of geese upon the lake
Maybe a mile long, thirty across—
Ten thousand curving forms repeating there.

Each gliding in its self-appointed place
Just barely touching side by feathered side,
Aglow, aglitter, incandescent in
The glorifying, unobstructed sun.

Who is this shimmering designed to please,
This fine effulgence of reflected light?
What kind of fabricator would contrive
This scene to help a witness like myself

Put darker, melancholy thoughts aside,
Thoughts of companions never to return,
Never to see migrating geese again—
The thrust of their stretched bodies blurred by flight

A sudden surge of black-tipped wings ascends
To startled tumult in the air, and I—
Lift up celebrating hands to join
This flourishing of animated sky.

WELCOMING FAREWELL

A cornucopia for winter birds,
our feeder welcomes nuthatches and chickadees
as snow ghosts hunker down in hemlock trees.
From silence they emerge which frames the words
we whisper in our fluted welcoming
to the arriving nuthatches and chickadees—
as if their coming is designed to please
our wish to share their company. And yet they bring
to mind the murmur of midsummer bees
that sparkled in a purple clover field.
The seasons merge as rumbling bees now yield
to snow ghosts silent in the hemlock trees
and we—attuned to disappearing wings,
the fluttering of nuthatches and chickadees,
the choiring harmony of honey bees,
their muted undertones, their murmurings—
we summon phrases of farewell to call
to the departing nuthatches and chickadees,
farewell to drowsy dragonflies and bees,
farewell to umber flare-up in effulgent fall,
in welcoming fresh silence that embraces bees,
embraces the translucent dragonfly, the whir
and thrum of the exhausted grasshopper,
and all quick nuthatches and chickadee.
bodes well for everyone.

NATIONAL BISON RANGE, MONTANA

Before the nineteenth century began
with the absurd assumption
Nature's resources are unlimited,
some sixty million bison grazed
the grasslands of our continent,
Western prairies stretched out
in the horizon's haze
where orange sunsets bleed
on snow-covered mountaintops.

Hunted by settlers and by Indians,
whole herds were soon exterminated;
in a hundred fleeting years
their desiccated skulls were stacked
in towers to witness their shared fate.
The wolves who preyed on bison calves,
the injured, or the frail,
suffered a loss of sustenance
as human populations grew
and prospered, and it only took
another hundred years before the bison,
terrified and fleeing, were then driven
over gaping precipices almost to
extinction's blank finality.

Their best survival strategy—
ironically in retrospect—
would have been to appeal
to homo sapiens, like wolves
who learned to guard our fires
in exchange for scraps of meat;
ten-thousand years ago they
morphed into domestic dogs.

Too big, not cute enough, and high
in protein, bison seemed destined to be
eliminated from the earth until
a savior, Teddy Roosevelt,
conceived the idea of a park
where bison could survive and multiply.

Call it a mystery—the reverence for life,
call it fortuitous, but something new
in the unfolding saga of
sustaining habitats—protecting,
peaceful, and secure—appeared
beneath the blaze of the indifferent sun—
a fabrication, mindfully designed—
deliberate and purposeful, and yet composed
only of water, earth, and air,
of seasons cycling and of leaves flashing
their effulgent colors in the wind.

So from this swooning height,
I look out at the flowing vistas
leading down steep rolling slopes
of incandescent yarrow fields,
each cluster of the tiny flowers
like miniature galaxies.
The swirl of space across a valley
winds to a river of smooth silver light
reflected from the current of the air
and radiates an inner silver of its own
before receding into azure shade.
There on the vaulted mountainside,
now shimmering with gold balsamroot
oblivious, composed, and still,
a dozen mighty bison graze;

among them bounds a tawny calf
as if it were the first calf ever born.

       A meadowlark is singing on the fence
that frames the border of the park,
expressing my heart's conviction
that this day with my own son,
with Pat and Dan, my cherished friends—
caretakers of the wilderness—
will end well.

BOBCAT AT HOLLAND LAKE LODGE

John was the longtime manager
of Holland Lodge
by pristine Holland Lake,
surrounded by the vast Swan Mountain Range
out to the east, and, to the west,
the mighty Mission Mountain Range.
If you look out across the lake,
you'll see an incandescent waterfall,
or if you row to the south shore.
it's likely you will see
gnawed branches heaped
above the waterline
to form the arched roof
of a beaver hutch.
You might spy white-tailed deer
descend past glinting pines
to drink at the lake's stony rim,
then pause to scrutinize
uncertain stirring in the underbrush.
High in a swaying tamarack,
an eagle settles in her nest
with folded wings.
You could be standing here
a quarter century ago,
the year my wife and I arrived,
and see what you see now:
unfurling purple clouds,
the ghostly sliver of a crescent moon,
a family of sleek Merganser ducks
dipping in ripples
of their buoyant element,
a painted turtle basking
on a partly sunken log.

You might imagine this tableau
had been designed by John
for every visitor's delight—
to be here without questioning,
just to observe, though it is tempting
to believe John's rapt description
of this hushed, encircled place as if
it were the Peaceable Kingdom
that Isaiah prophesied.

   One languid summer day
when I was reading by the lake,
John unexpectedly appeared
cradling a baby bobcat at his chest.
John made a blanket bed for him
inside the cabin where he lived
behind the public lodge;
and also built a cage outside
from which the bobcat could
peer out into the spangled woods
and sniff the currents of the wind.

   Though he resembled a domestic cat,
when he attained maturity,
his shoulder tendons tightened
and the muscles in his back
became more taut and sinewy.

   I felt primeval power
lurking everywhere I touched.
On snowy afternoons, I'd sit
cross-legged upon the cabin floor,
and he would slink up from behind,
set his spread paws upon my back
and rub his cheek against my cheek
as if to reassure me
of our creature-bond.

John's son had cautioned me
that stalking was the way
bobcats hunt hares and rodents
they depend upon for sustenance.
A bobcat will attack a hare
with silent steps upon the snow;
one pounce is needed, nothing more.
    John had informed me that
it was his plan from the beginning
when he brought the baby bobcat home
to set him loose to find a mate
in the remaining wilderness.
    "But what if he can't make it
in the wild?" I queried John.
"What if we have smothered
his ancestral instinct to survive?"
My apprehension must have troubled John
since it took years before, at mating time,
he set the bobcat free.
    In March the Lodge was emptied of its quests,
and John could travel anywhere he wished
although he chose to keep
his destination to himself.
    A couple that my wife and I
befriended way back in our city days
had come for a reunion at our house.
"We haven't watched the sun
reflected on a mountain peak—
not since our honeymoon,"
his wife lamented to my wife
beside the consolation of a fire
the snowfall night that they arrived.
    Next day I drove them the
few rutted miles to Holland Lake
to contemplate the spectral radiance

of the half-frozen waterfall,
when at the forest's birch-grove borderline,
    I spied our bobcat crouching on a rock.
My friends could see me looking, so
they saw the bobcat too
as he charged toward us
at ferocious speed. Not breaking stride,
yet catching the effulgent light,
the bobcat leapt into my outstretched arms
as a reverberating scream
surged from my friends in unison
who clung together by
the ice-encrusted lake as if
this were their second honeymoon.
    "That's how wild animals respond to me!"
I oratorically proclaimed
to comfort my astounded friends
that legendary day
as if Isaiah's prophecy
had finally been realized.
John never did return
to Holland Lodge;
he was succeeded by his son
who had the bobcat's cage removed,
yet laughed approvingly to hear my tale
about a forest animal
who had remembered who I was,
inspiring me to utter words
that might well serve
to sound the trumpet of my epitaph—
my celebration of a peaceful
kingdom's glistening.

GRIEVING FOR ANNIE

When we behold a wide turf-covered expanse, we should
remember that its smoothness, on which so much of its
beauty depends, is mainly due to the inequalities having
been slowly leveled by worms.

—CHARLES DARWIN

Prolific Darwin is remembered for
his ailments and his generosity
toward loyal friends, consideration for
his wife's life-long religious faith,
devotion to his many children,
Annie in particular, who died
of fever at the age of ten.
        Darwin's commitment to the truth
of how Nature designed itself, based on
observation and analysis.
Evidence, despite the consolation
offered by a Christian after-life
that needed to be given up, provides
a model for the tolerant of stomach
and the unequivocal of heart.
        Darwin's great theory of selection and
Descent how creatures struggle to compete
since their supplies of food are limited—
is the most powerful idea ever
conceived by humankind because
of its explanatory scope and depth:
we all remain at heart what once we've been.
Species will flourish in their time,

become extinct when circumstances change,
and vanish never to return again—
a truth excruciating to accept.

Darwin thought evolution had produced
"forms beautiful and wonderful."
The "war of Nature" was a process
he described as having "grandeur"
since increased complexity had led
in time to human consciousness,
society, and moral sentiments
like sympathy, benevolence, and trust.
    But Darwin's attitude about how
Nature operated to select the fit
kept darkening until, disburdening
himself of pent-up anguish, Darwin
wrote to Joseph Hooker, his good friend,
condemning Nature's works as "clumsy,
wasteful, blundering, and horrible;"
no consolation for inevitable
conflict can be found except perhaps
through human care and tenderness,
the pleasure that we sometimes take
in bringing pleasure to someone we love
as little Annie surely did for him.
He wrote an elegy extolling her,
"It was delightful to behold her face,"
recording her last quaint and gracious words
as "I quite thank you" when he held
her head and offered her a final drink.
    And yet it's dubious that evolution
can account for such unselfishness
or tell him where to look for consolation
in a world where loss, unmerited
and indiscriminate, seems absolute
beyond repair or recompense.
Surviving Annie's stupefying death
Darwin continued to be burdened by
the marble weight of mournfulness,

and yet he went on working since his work
allowed for self-forgetfulness
and granted him the patience to endure.
    Twenty outreaching years after her death
Darwin composed a book in praise of worms,
comparing them to gardeners who
"prepare the ground for seedlings of all kinds,"
depicting worms as cultivators—first
among the farmers of the earth.
    Did Darwin find some consolation in
the laboring of lowly worms who plowed
the soil for ages immemorial
in knowledge of renewal through decay?
Could such relief suffice for him
and ease the ache of his undying grief?

EPITHALAMIUM

Early in March, Erik my son, and I,
and Dan and Pat, caretakers
of the wilderness, set forth
to view Montana's Freezeout Lake
where thousands of Snow Geese
stop off to rest and feed before
continuing their journey north.
    Astonished, with long arms outstretched
like a Blue Heron's coasting wings,
Dan watched sleek geese descend
in dense coordinated swoops, then circle
and return to the illuminated lake;
together we observed the Tundra Swans
glide silently as if they knew
they were admired by us
and need not hasten to depart
as long as their suffusing glow
ignited our own flowing thoughts.
    Before our transfixed eyes
the streaking swans seemed motionless
as if composed in a tableau
arranged that instant as
an unrepeatable design,
like the design that brought us here,
our mutual delight in spectacle.
    We marveled how their pattern
constantly revived itself
until the moment came for them
to fade away on their illuminated wings,
departing from our sight
that migratory season in
its swirling Freezeout interval.

Collective awe had bonded us anew
so that in time and telling
being there and being gone
will not be seen as separate
when once again we share accounts
of how the incandescent swans
propelled black-footed bodies up
from the reverberating lake.

        Remembered springtime merges into now,
and now we gather here to celebrate—
full summer humming in our bones—
the promises of loyalty
encircling what elusive time
makes precious in the urgency
of knowing that we must at last
relinquish everything we love
to the indifferent air.

        Briefly among us congregated
on the breeding earth, we come, we go,
along with plants, with trees, with birds,
with butterflies, with animals—
Pat's shiny- eyed-endangered Pikas
huddled on the Glacier mountaintop,
guardians at the border where
protecting cold is needed
for their pulsing bodies to survive.

        And now vermillion light bears witness
to our witnessing, this wedding feast—
the vows that carry us beyond ourselves
in this suspended interval
like the ascent of disappearing swans,
even beyond what we can see.
As you, dear friends, are unified
by consecrated words, so are we all;
with our winged words we're able to

make manifest the rapturous idea
of fellowship, fulfilling right here
in this cherished place of keeping watch,
of water mirroring the mountains
and the sky, what we, alive,
have always wished—that our own wilderness
of fertile wishes may endure and thrive.

MEADOWLARK

A view to set against oblivion,
Gold-blooming balsamroot illuminates
The mountainside and circumscribes the one
Noteworthy, preening meadowlark who waits

For my approval then begins again
As if his melody within my mind
Is also needed by grouped angels when
They are assembled listening to find

Heavenly satisfaction in a sight
So season-bound and so ephemeral
In the contingency of golden light
Made manifest in a bird's lilting call

Resounding through the vibrant April air
Complete and ultimate, just being there.

INCREDIBLE BEAR ENCOUNTER

I took an unfamiliar path
into the tangled wilderness.
the elevation higher, and the air
just thin enough to make
my breathing somewhat difficult
and cause my intermittent view
of the vast Mission mountain range,
the valley plummeting below,
to seem a hazy blue in swirling light.

I stumbled on a fallen branch
and think I may have hit my head.
as from behind a vaulting pine
a giant grizzly bear appeared
who reared upright in front of me,
his sickle claws stretched out,
saliva dripping from his teeth.

I know you can't outrun a bear,
and though I am an atheist,
I figured that my only chance was prayer.
"Lord!" I exclaimed, my face
raised heavenward,
"If You will intervene to spare my life,
protect me from this mighty bear,
I promise that I'll read the bible with
an open mind right to its scary end;
I'll make a generous donation to
The Wilderness Society;
I'll be more sensitive in choosing
whom to tell offensive jokes."

"Not too convincing," I acknowledged
to myself, yet that's the best
I could come up with on the spot.
The bear took one step closer,

stared at me, then lifted up his eyes
to scan the sky, and in a language
I, incredibly, could comprehend,
he said "I thank you. Lord for this fine meal,
this blessing that Your bounty is
about to graciously bestow on me."
      That very instant all the leaves,
the aspens and the cottonwoods,
stopped quaking and went absolutely still;
the nearby stream ceased tumbling in its flow;
a pillaged woodpecker desisted
in his echoed hammering;
clouds thickened, and the sky closed in.
      I realized I could not emulate
the bear's sincerity
and that I had to improvise
a more persuasive strategy.
But I know nothing of the purposes
a deity might have in mind
in making all-consuming hunger
the first, universal motive
of all living things, or why chance is
a factor in the way events turn out.
      But knowing that I do not know is all I could be certain of.
If someone up there might be listening,
it's sure that he or maybe she wants to remain inscrutable,
and what can possibly
be more inscrutable, I thought,
than my escaping from this bear
or that the bear should suddenly
turn peaceable? And so, content
with my intrepid reasoning,
I felt secure that I could rest my case.
      When I awoke, the aspen leaves
again were quaking in the wind;

the stream was foaming over purple stones;
the woodpecker resumed his hammering,
but on the tree above my head,
illuminated in a lunar beam,
I saw a silver tuft of fur
where the great bear had rubbed his back,
perhaps to ease a sudden itch, and then
had disappeared into the underbrush.
Incredible as it may seem,
I felt a pang of apprehension in the bear's behalf:
for how in hell
can he survive, with his gigantic appetite,
unless he has enough to eat?

SNOW SCENE WITH RAVEN

Wet clinging snow accumulates
On aspen branches, birches, tamaracks,
On cedar fences that delineate
The silent fields, the frozen stalks

and barren brambles that express
the tangle of what shapes remain.
Whiteness, unifying whiteness,
Extends, diffuses, and contains.

The icy dazzle of its glittterings.
An interrupting raven clamors past,
Its gold eye vivid in a blur of wings;
This pang of darkness cannot last.

I'm here where all temptations come to go,
Enraptured in oblivion of snow.

BEAR GRASS INTERVAL

At roughly ten year intervals
this globe of minuscule white flowers
clustered on a dense green stalk
appears profusely in the vernal woods
of mountain-range Montana,
so the entranced observer stares
at what appears to be
a galaxy of stars that has now drifted down
and settled softly on the earth.
    Ask anybody who has witnessed
this phantasmagorical display,
and they will swear
that they have never seen
a spectacle so tranquil
and serenely beautiful.
    Yet I imagine beauty
here on earth does not
originate in the beholder's eye,
but dwells out there inherent
 in the humming universe
as one of Plato's fundamental forms
beyond the realm of time and space
that still can harmonize discordant thought
and woo the tides of the recumbent air.
    You ask how this far-out belief
affects my life; am I
less self-absorbed and less defined
by personal diminishing
to primal and concluding nothingness?
    Perhaps if everyone would pause
to gaze upon the Bear Grass flowers
glowing on the mountainside,
and view them as if willfully designed,

a combination of sweet symmetries
and startling randomness,
then they would feel less separate,
less lonely, less irrelevant, content
to play the quiet role of witnesses.
 But now, right now, the galaxy
of Bear Grass flowers is not visible
 and will not reappear
for an uncertain interval,
assuming earthly time
still measures disappearances,
the emptiness lost love and friendship leave
forever achingly behind.
 I do not know if I'll endure
another interval—a wandering
beholder of the momentary woods—
until Bear Grass returns to grace my sight
and holds there, astounded
and suspended in delight.

WATER MEMORIES, WATER DREAMS

When I was twenty-one
and hiking up a mountainside
to reach a waterfall
a girl walked with me.
We were holding hands although
I did not try to kiss her, thinking
that she might reject my overture.
Her mind unknown to me,
we sat together on a fallen tree,
watching the waterfall spin out its foam
above the darker current underneath,
forever changing, always the same,
constant in its inconstancy.

Years floated by, and resting on a ledge
above a swimming hole gouged out
by a cascading stream,
I saw a father with his son
appear and leap together
 in the churning pool. At once
the father was sucked down
although he managed to thrust up
his writhing son above his head
so I was able to grab hold of him
and host him safely back on land.
The father disappeared so rapidly
I couldn't find him when
I dove in after him. His body
was recovered the next day
bolt upright in a whirling vortex
with his arms outstretched as if
he still were beckoning for help.

Another outpouring of years,
and there I am canoeing in a cove
observing feeding ducks dip down
then shake themselves and preen,
their shimmering green heads
resplendent in mid- summer sun.
I strip down to my underwear,
slither into the lake and swim across,
not caring how I will get back.

One umber fall I walk out on our dock
to watch the geese in wedged formation
test their wings in preparation for
their migratory journey south.
I look down at still water and I see
my own reflection in the lake;
a sweat drop from my forehead falls
and ripples outward from my face
as if intending to reveal
a purposeful design.

To this day I still dream
in water images, and I suspect I may
have once been rescued from the sea
when I was maybe two years old—
the summer that my parents
rented a log cabin by the shore
according to my mother's memory.
I asked her if she let me play
in the wet sand collecting shells
among the skittering of sandpipers,
but all she let herself recall
was that my father was not well
and that she had to care for him.

Again last night I had a swimming dream.
Too far from land, I felt
the pulsing of the universal tide
and felt the ocean rise as when
first separated from the firmament.

I woke abruptly from the dream
with curled waves unfurling at my back
and ventured forth into the hazy air,
into the rain that falls
upon the rich and on the poor,
upon the young and on the old,
on women as on men,
on all the virtuous, all the corrupt,
on humans and on animals,
upon the joyous and the sorrowful,
skeptics, believers, and the searchers
who are certain only of uncertainty:
all are alike at heart, including me—
we all are interchangeable, and so
without complaint, without regret.
without some distant place to go.
I have no wish my life were otherwise.

HUMMING IN THE AIR,
FLUTE MUSIC ON LAND

I'm drifting slowly in my wooden boat,
observing turtles sunning on a log,
seeing how close I can approach
before they plunk, like a plucked violin,
into the lake and disappear.

I shiver with the pleasure
of just being here, measuring
my afternoon in turtle intervals
of vanishing—when suddenly
my disappearing turtle trance
is interrupted by the thrumming
of a streaking heron's wings
and my heart's pulse becomes
the down strokes of extended wings.

I sense a soft vibration in the air
as if a choir were humming
in a cloud, an intimation
at the core of quietude.

My boat glides closer to the shore
and I can hear a tanager's faint trill
passing so quickly that I am not sure
it really fluttered there
in shifting intermittent shade.

Murmuring ripples on the lake waft in
and then the swoosh of wind
among a canopy of pines.
descends and settles in the underbrush.

And I am wondering
what my rapt presence adds
as I pause here between
those painted turtles on their log
and their swift vanishing
into their silent element.
between the heron's flashing
and its blur diminishing beyond
the blue horizon's borderline.

Perhaps our evanescent universe,
red-shifted to infinity,
requires a listener,
a wide-eyed observer, someone
to behold his own beholding here,
right here beneath our minor sun.

There on the pebbled shore,
a flute raised to her lips,
a slender barefoot lady stands
about to play, and playing,
and already having played,
her silver notes float toward me over
glintings on the surface of the lake.

Mellifluous, they flow as if
intending to make music mean
much more than meaning
ever previously meant—
repeatably repeatable,
like circles in their circularity,
serene, and permanent.

SWAN RIVER IN OCTOBER

Shimmering crimson clouds
are now reflected on the river as
my son and I coast downstream
toward no destination
in particular. We paddle and we drift,
feeling the current in our bones,
repeating its inevitable flow.
Ahead we see a beaver lodge
fringed with fresh branches harvested
for winter nourishment to feed
a family of six or more. A beaver
slaps the water with its thick, flat tail
which makes a cracking sound
that echoes like a rifle shot.
And high above, three Sandhill cranes
in silhouette, with wing-spans
almost eight feet long, prepare
for immanent migration south,
forming a triangle which they maintain
until they have diminished out of sight.
A rainbow trout with its pink stripe
breaks through the surface calm to snatch a bug,
creating ripples that dissolve
expanding into circles so symmetrical
one might imagine a designer
improvised in forms that no competitor
would presume to emulate.
My son avoids a tree stump
lurking just beneath the mirror
of configured clouds, and I can see
a vein jump in his sun-burned neck
as he swerves our wood-carved canoe
back on its course to somewhere

still to be decided as late light
begins to settle in the reeds
and in the berry-studded shrubbery.
A doe arrives at river's edge
and adds her hoof prints to the tell-tale mud;
she bows her head to drink,
then suddenly lifts up as water
tumbles from her lips; her ears twitch as
she stares in our direction though,
assuringly, I whisper we
have no desire to cause her harm—
all creatures here are safe for now—
but, unpersuaded, off she goes
into the rustling underbrush.

    And now I wonder what my son
might say to me, or I to him,
beside our tended fire tonight
within a ring of gathered stones;
does something all-fulfilling
and definitive require expression
in our human words, or can
our drifting on Swan River with
reflected cloud formations twice
glimpsed in their darkened colors I
cannot describe, sustain us
and inscrutably suffice.

PASTRAMI IN PARADISE

Zabars may well be the best Jewish
delicatessen in New York.

Now that I have late leisure time to spend,
I'm able freely to meander
among cloudy speculations whether
in some frequented neighborhood
in paradise one still can order
a pastrami sandwich on rye bread.
And drowsily I wonder if my mother,
having settled in for the long haul,
still makes heroic matzah balls
to celebrate the holidays.
    I can remember her dyslexia,
how she'd confuse the names
of the male members in our family
and call me Carl, my father's name,
or call her grandson (on my sister's side)
Bobby, yet every one of us was certain
to reply when summoned by her.
    I recollect the day when Jamie
told her that the Peace Corps offered him
a full-year's fellowship to study
tribal rituals in Africa, and, anxious
to the marrow of her Jewish bones,
she phoned me to inquire
what foods the natives eat in Africa:
"Isn't starvation a big problem there?"
"But where in Africa," I questioned her,
"has Jamie been assigned?"
"It's a huge continent." She paused,
and then she answered, "Zabars, I think
Zabars is where they're sending him." "That's good,"
I cheerfully replied, "there's nothing then

for you to fear; he'll come back home
at least a few pounds heavier."
    A half a century has failed to dim
this vivid memory, and now
I'm wondering if the distracted Lord
enjoys a saucy anecdote like this
with its intrigue of interchanging names.
And when my mother's turn comes round
to stand before the holy throne,
will she repeat the questions
that disturbed her mortal days?
    Will she, in her dyslexic innocence,
address the Lord as Joseph, her
own father's name—Joseph
who never let his tea grow cold—
to ask if loss, her husband's early death,
somehow had been required
in the elusive scheme of things
for her love to attain full vigilance?
    On her refrigerator door, as if
engraved in stone, my mother pinned these words:
IN TIMES OF HAPPINESS, EAT HEARTILY;
WHEN SORROW COMES, ALSO EAT HEARTILY.
I see her in her comfortable shoes
and the white apron that my grandma wore;
she hands the Lord a sandwich for His lunch—
pastrami with a pickle on rye bread.
"Ess! ess!" she urges Him, "I know You still
have cares that need revisiting."

SANDHILL CRANES DANCING

At dawn the Sandhill cranes, their heads
splashed vivid red, initiate
their mating dance, circling each other
on long, narrow legs tanning their huge, gray wings
in slow, dreamlike deliberation.
    They throw sticks from their pointed beaks
into the air to flaunt their mating skills.
Their whooping echoes out across
the same dew-sparkled field
where they've returned each spring
for twenty years since we, my wife and I,
initially began to keep our watch.
    A forest ranger we'd not met before
stops by our house to ask if we have seen
the grizzly bear tracks in the mud
beside our border stream. He tells us that
the constellation Ursa Major will
appear tonight effulgent
right above us in the northern sky
and that he likes to stay awake at night,
with just his telescope for company,
to calculate how long it takes
red-shifted light to reach the earth.
"My favorite is melancholy Saturn,"
he declares and its attendant moons,
each one with its own orbit, hue, and size.
My hope is that I'll find a hidden moon
that no one has observed before;
it would preserve my name."
    He says that stars right now are being born
and burning out, collapsing on themselves,
that due to universal entropy
in maybe fifty-million years

all matter will thin out and dissipate,
so that no memory and no
intelligence—none would survive.

    And even I, who own no telescope,
can comprehend terminal emptiness;
it's no less thinkable than is
next May without our being here to watch
the cranes perform their dance as if
their tossing sticks into the dawn
and catching them might signify
that everything returns again
to re-enact past happiness.

    Yet in our bones we know that soon
our bearing witness must conclude,
just as the green field must turn brown,
which it, alas, has been designed to do.
So let us pause again in misty light
to watch those red crests blur and disappear
above the waving trees. and listen hard
as medleyed crane calls float away
and fade into a murmur in the air.

PERFECT RAINBOW

    Driving me home from yet
another visit to the eye doctor,
my wife took the old farmland route,
and there across a field of corn,
stretching from east to west,
a rainbow's arc appeared;
uninterrupted and connecting
earthbound base to earthbound base,
its glowing colors merging yet distinct,
perfectly symmetrical, it shimmered there
ascending heavenward, descending back.
I wondered how I might regard
this biblical display, the admonition
from Leviticus requiring us to leave
unharvested a measure of the crop
at the designated far edge
for the unfortunate and destitute.

    Before my tearing eyes, the field of corn,
swayed by a sudden surge of wind
became transformed into a roiling sea,
and I looked out, as Noah had,
to see a perfect rainbow beckoning,
assuring him dry land would soon appear,
that life would long continue for his wife,
his sons, the coupled animals.

    But then the rainbow disappeared
behind accumulating clouds,
and my imagining myself as Noah
dissipated into evening gloom.
though I imagined ragged figures
crouching at the border of the field.

I wondered whether Noah wondered
what vicissitudes awaited him
 and his attending family
when he descended from the ark,
what fate awaited all those animals,
who no longer would be in his care.

    When we arrived back home again,
my wife helped me into our house where I
could rest beside the animated fire
of red and yellow flickering.
My dog lay his moist nose upon my feet;
my cat leaped to my lap, curled up,
and purred as if she were in paradise.
Lightning lit up our windows with a flash;
thunder resounded in the rafter beams,
and it began to pour in silver waves
as rampant wind besieged the trees
and pounded hail stones in the flower beds
although the house itself felt water-tight.

    My wife rushed over to the kitchen door
and opened it against invading wind
as, two by two, the animals came in
and shook themselves: the white-tailed deer,
foxes and wolves, red squirrels, bobcats,
beavers, otters, skunks, and antelope,
and quail and grouse, turkeys and short-eared owls,
and, yes, of course, brown bears came too,
and thick-necked grizzlies with their mighty claws.
"It must have been the rainbow," my wife said.

Event Horizon
(2021)

☾

OBOE SERENADE

Abiding comforters
renew thy comforting—
the mountain's wind-stirred choruses,
the echoings of loons
across the lake,
their overflowing water notes
uplifted among the swaying tamaracks,
the lilting lake's curved repetitions
of the crescent moon.

How long ago
did hooting of the loons
become transformed to brooding blue?

We are not made for happiness
which fades out when inklings of oblivion begin.
We hear reverberating music
linger in its dwindled aftermath.

The flowing oboe sounds of loons
merge with the mountain's shifting shades,
the lake's lugubrious blue murmurings.
And I—suspended
in abounding blue—I could be anyone,
I could be you.

SCULPTING AN ELEPHANT

From the dust, in his own image, Yahweh
created humankind.
I think that he was lonely, that the need
for company was on his mind.

After he made the animals,
he showed them first to Adam just to see
what he would name them to complete
their physical identity.

Inspired to sculpt a life-size elephant,
I ordered from Carrara, Italy,
for all the money I had saved as guide
at the museum of ancient history,

a massive chunk of marble stone
from which to make my masterpiece
with great reality to emulate,
desire for form that will not cease.

And so I planned to chip away
all the surrounding shapeless stone,
thus freeing Plato's ideal elephant
beyond mere muscle, flesh and bone.

I leaned my ladder up against the stone,
so I could swing my mallet easily,
and soon a hint of curve revealed
what in concentrated time would be

the smooth slope of a hip, and then,
a deep-ridged forehead and thin, wrinkled ears,
a steep, protruding brow shows forth, and then
the first sign of a trunk appears.

I carve the trunk stretched out
to send his trumpet message that
this is my ancestral territory,
my protected habitat.

I reach out and my ladder tips,
and I come crashing to the floor.
The trunk is broken off. I'll start again,
with less aspiring to be more.

So my aesthetic principle
becomes verisimilitude
with likeness an implicit aura,
an insinuated mood,

objective and yet personal,
with vaulting thick-set legs to rest upon
like the prodigious columns
of the aspiring Parthenon.

And now I can recall the down-home cure
Aristotle prescribed for shoulder pain
in elephants: rub with warmed vinegar
till only pleasure throbs remain.

And thus for a brief moment
underneath the firmament,
there is no loneliness,
no unfulfilled intent.

Creature, creator—both as one—
are what I must affirm
to realize myself
renamed a packyderm.

OUR LONG HOME
(after Ecclesiastes)

Remember well your body's proud delights
In supple youth, the aged rabbi says,

Before the days close in when you
Take little pleasure in their shimmering,

Before your thin arms tremble,
Your teeth now unable to chew meat,

Before the windows of your eyes grow dim,
And all you see outside is mist,

Before your voice won't carry
In the clamor of the street

Where mourners congregate,
And children stop to gaze at them,

Before your private door is shut,
And you can't venture to the countryside

To hear the trilling of meadowlark
The bluebird's whispered twittering,

Before you stumble when you walk,
And every pebble is an obstacle,

Before no soft wind carries
The aroma of a cherry tree's white blossoming,

Before the whirring of a grasshopper
Fails to commemorate your pausing in a field,

Before the cord that holds your spine erect
Loosens and finally lets go,

Before your potter's bowl of thoughts,
your pitcher of fond sentiments,

Is shattered on the rim-stones of the well
Where often you have paused to rest.

The hour now nears for your return to dust
The dust from which you first arose,

The same dust that you share with all the animals,
The noble lion and the lowly worm—

All speechless and without possessions,
Nothing to relinquish or regret—

With whom you'll share your long home
In the silent earth, the cruel and the meek,

The swift and slow, the unjust and the just,
The weak, the powerful—all now the same,

All now are one. And so, my son, you must accept
What is beyond control, beyond your first and final wish.

Life is a shadow of a shade,
The blink of a reflection in a drop of dew,

Breath adding exhaled breath to emptiness,
So briefly that we wonder whether we were here.

Yet here we are, knowing that Sorrow opens up the heart
To strangers as it does to friends,

To the abandoned and bereaved—
All, all alike in their distress,

All in ongoing need of comforting,
Of solace in the unbeholding dark.

Carry your lamp among the fireflies,
Your nearest stars that guide the way

To being right here where you are;
 Cherish your gift for cherishing,

For light is soothing, light is sweet,
the changing hues and colors

Of autumnal leaves are welcome
To blurred eyes even in winter memory,

The yellows deepening to gold
And burnished gold to deeper bronze

With luscious reds, effulgent oranges,
Luxuriating in their afterglow.

DARWIN'S LAST BEETLE

Ah well, Dear Helpmate, just compare
 our troubles in this gated world
at home here dwelling where we are
ephemeral in sun, in rain,
with those of Darwin and his wife.
Emma, unwavering, believed
that Jesus was her savior and
assuredly would bring her up
to heaven when her days with earth
as home were over and complete.

The problem for her Christian faith
was Charles' theory about how
we human beings had evolved
entirely by Nature's laws,
like universal gravity,
and not divine creation by
a loving God. Such new ideas
were blasphemous and without hope
and might well make impossible
admittance into Paradise.
The thought they'd spend the afterlife
apart, alone, tormented her.
Can Paradise without dear Charles
be Paradise as promised her?
Did God not fashion Eve to fill
the wound of Adam's loneliness?

Charles thought that Nature can produce
new forms, designs most beautiful,
the wooing ornaments of birds,
the higher animals, and yet
the cruelty of natural
processes and phenomena,
famine, and bloody appetite,

and struggle went on without end.
  "A Devil's Chapbook," he once wrote,
would list Nature's atrocities.

      Rapturous in boyhood, wholly
distracted and absorbed, Darwin
roamed meadows, hills, and fields to search
for beetles he could add to his
collection's worldly treasury.
Beetle questing I understand,
and his comparing finches' beaks
far off in the Galapagos.
But what have I, a skeptic Jew,
to offer Emma—I who can't
contend with pissed-off Yahweh who
tells me (check out Leviticus)
that I have fallen short of his
severe demand for holiness,
concern for all the desolate,
the unrequited and the poor.
As for The Ten Commandments, well,
not coveting for me is still
the very hardest to obey
because it's wholly in the mind.

      In the last year of his long life
of illness, disability
that still cannot be diagnosed,
and studying his "farmer" worms,
how they can cultivate the soil,
Darwin received a specimen
for his astute analysis:
A water beetle with his legs
caught in the grip of a grim clam.
But on arrival in the mail,
the beetle somehow freed itself,
though it was weakened and had lost

its vital animating strength.
Charles put it in a bottle with
some chopped up laurel leaves that oozed
a substance like an opiate
to soothe the beetle's suffering
and ease its speechless creature-way
to empty, everlasting death.

   But here, my own dear helpmate pal,
the rosy apple of my eye,
temptress, cajoler, my spared rib—
here is a bright epiphany,
my gift to your forbearing heart.
Right here in the confounding dark,
picture the whole admissions board
for entry into Paradise
as bleary rabbi angels
with their cloaks as wings, their yamalkas
as shaded in dim candlelight.
All are Talmudic exegetes.
Unanimously, they agree
Charles Darwin should be granted a
full membership in Paradise
as his deserved award for his
wondrously magnanimous,
species-transcending empathy,
to be with beloved Emma up above,
where no doubt, I might safely add,
astonishing varieties
of beetles trippingly abound
amid the fields and tangled banks
to be collected and arranged,
neatly in rows, each one in place
distinctive in its own design,
preserved for all eternity.

SATAN ADDRESSES THE U.N.

My fellow warriors for peace,
can rebel power of the powerful
redeem rebellion in our minds?
I'm grateful for your invitation to
address you this evening on
the fundamental theme of blame.
My goal is to make easier
your often unappreciated work
by clarifying the first principles
of my own contribution as
the tempter with the wish for power and
for unnatural immortality.
Since humans are composed of dust,
I need to make sure that they do get the blame
for all the suffering that will
inevitably follow from
a cause they were not author of.

Original conditions like
the "Apple Trick," humbly I must confess,
which was my own, my very best idea
since Adam really didn't know enough—
how to resist temptation's trap
without possessing first the knowledge that
the apple subsequently would provide.
Too late! Essential knowledge comes too late!
Exactly as I had contrived,
insinuating subtly as a snake,
I knew the guilt would fall on him and her.
Blaming each other, they became
the model for all future strife:
nation against nation, sect against sect,
theology against theology.
Self-righteous, they would only see
in time to come their hatred in

the hatred of their enemies.
And I got Adam even to blame God.
"The woman whom You gave me," Adam snarled,
"she tempted me, and I did eat."
Autumnal leaves in Eden that first year
turned brown and dry and drifted to the ground.

    I like a world with good in it—
in which misfortune strikes the innocent,
lavish cruelty goes unpunished,
and sorrow sets its vigil in the brain.
All living things must eat to live, must kill.
I don't know how it could be otherwise.

    And yet on unexpected days as if
in fiery rebellion from myself,
I feel a pulsing throb of pity for
the wretched, the abandoned, the abused,
even the lonely, even the despised.
The widow slinks from the dark alleyway
into her dim room in the slums.
The hungry child stares into vacancy.
The rapist flicks his silver blade and waits
in lurking shadows underneath the bridge.
In the untended park, the addict hides
his needle from his fellows there.
Beyond the gate, in a red shirt,
the organ grinder's monkey holds his cup
out to the passers-by who, heads down, are
hurrying somewhere out of sight.
Someone's to blame for all this misery.
There's got to be a cause; someone has got
to take the blame, but you don't have to blame yourselves.

    There always are the Jews to blame.
We have abundant precedent for that:
Lending and buying they control the banks.

But you have heard the money slur before.
You'd think they'd just been freed from servitude
in Egypt yesterday to claim the land
they say their God had promised them.
Wars have been fought, grave after grave,
to civilize disputed land,
and they believe their jealous God
will "circumcise their hearts"
in order to renew their covenant.

    I do not know what this strange image means,
but it sounds ominous to me—
a threat portending an apocalypse.
Perhaps there is a mystery
about the human heart, what it desires,
that I don't understand—maybe it is
the wish to taste the apple glowing from
that other garden tree with its
forbidden immortality,
to live forever and become
an innocent and blameless deity.

    Maybe it is no more than a wish
to find endurable, acceptable,
decaying nature as it is,
unable to undream the dream of peace,
including childbirth, servitude,
including labor, and including grief.

PAUL MARIANI LAUGHING

OK, Paulo, I then said, here's another Jewish joke
in which bodily awareness—
that one might call a mitzvah of the flesh—
outlasts high-mindedness.
Leave behind the aspiration
to transcend our creaturehood.

So brace yourself, make firm your touchas
on your leather chair. If you have gleeful groans for me,
prepare to moan them now.
They will be music to my ears.

A Buddhist priest asserts that what we call
"the self," our agent of identity,
is merely an illusion,
nothing more than empty wind.
The priest's companion, Rabbi Solomon,
holds up his blue-veined hands,
and he replies, "If no such thing as 'self' exists,
Oy veh, whose arthritis can this be?"

Paul chuckles, then his chuckle opens to a laugh,
his laugh into the heave of a guffaw.
He tumbles toward me,
and I catch him wholly in a hug,
then I'm guffawing too;
I'm shaking out of all control.
He hugs me back, his great bear body
caught up in the whirling of a dance—
a sinous symphonic creature dance.
And though we're bonded here on earth,
we see our laughing selves float upwards,
hands and feet and touchases and heads—
up, up beyond all body ache,
of thinking about absence, grieving about loss.

Only our airy laughter still abides.
buoyant melody, surpassing words.
My dear Paulo, the music of our being here together
in this vertigo of western light:

Paired trombones wail,
reverberating in the purple hills,
their mellow tones made mellower in unison.
Bassoon arpeggios, like loon calls,
merge with oboe owl hoots
all along the foaming borders of the lake.
Round double bass notes
resonate their thrum to welcome wanderers—
whoever, needful, might attend
to listen to the music of our airy laughter,
and, selflessly, in tune with us,
remain in harmony a while.

GOING BLIND

This dark is not the dark that nature meant
To ease me softly into dreamless sleep.
After my rebel talent has been spent,
After there is no inner light to keep.

My protestations turn from bad to verse,
Trapped in this sonnetorium, my life.
My ironies are rusty, puns get worse,
Attempting to amuse my friends, my wife.

Perhaps Promethean blind hope can save
My somber spirits in this mirthless dark,
Revive the stony promise of the grave
Where last comes first—zebra becomes aardvark.

I'll serve martinis outside heaven's gate
To those in doubt who only stand and wait.

WHITENESS

Wet snow accumulates
on pines, on firs,
on spruce, on tamaracks,
on broken stalks
and twisted shrubbery;
it eases down
on fields, on hills,
on mountain slopes,
on ice-locked riverbanks,
on shingled roofs
of slanting barns,
on cedar fences
and on perching ravens' wings,
the backs of browsing horses
and on stationary elk.

Heaped snow accumulates
upon heaped snow
this muffled afternoon
as a lone man,
snow clinging to his cap,
his eyelashes,
stomps heavily among the looming trees;
he is oblivious
to why he wanders there
with all the shades
of whiteness—all
its tints and hues and glimmerings
now merging almost imperceptibly,
dissolving into one.

ICICLE

Mid-January thaw extends the moonlit icicle
descending from my window eave.
It's not yet dawn, and I stand here
and stare at a latched gate
that opens on a gravel path
that leads across a field
with dry leaves blowing on the crust of snow
that dwindle and then disappear.

A figure pauses at the gate
perhaps deciding whether to return or to delay.
Three ravens huddle on the cedar fence,
their black sheen radiating in the air
in warning of the coming day.

A surge of wind unlatches
the closed gate, and I can hear
it knock against its post
as if, enraptured in my place,
I hear the heartbeat of a ghost.

I'm drowsy from my interrupted sleep,
and I suppose the figure stalking there might be
my father's ghost returning at long last
to finish what he had left unresolved—
forgiving his own brother's stealing from their partnership
that left him, only at a guess,
with the wide field and its adjacent wilderness.

Slowly the ghost approaches,
though he glances back, so I'm reminded of
long rows of apple trees along a hill
with sheep and horses
in the summer light
grazing according to their will.

The door swings closed behind him as
he reaches out to me,
and I, unable to respond,
imagine that he has
a pruning shears in hand,
or maybe it's a gun,
but I suspect he still is dazed by grief,
and I suspect he could be anyone.

I do not know
if his sole brother still
has claims on the disputed property
or if he now has children of his own
as his inheritors, not me.

I want to ask my father if a man
in time can learn how to accept
what's unacceptable,
but he's still not prepared to say,
to speak of the unspeakable,
except in what his haunted looks and gestures can convey.

He reaches out to me again,
and instantly the sun leaps up
behind the hooded mountaintop
and blazes in the icicle that drips,
like human tears, drop after drop.

MERGING

Sorrow and laughter merge as one
when she plays on her gleaming flute
in flowing cadences.
Her melody recalls
who we once were, pours forth
who we are now,
who we may yet become.
I picture her posed in a forest glade,
reflected in a lily pond,
partly in sunlight,
partly in liquid shadows
rippling over her bare shoulders,
over loosened hair.
Low languid clouds hold summer in
their frothy radiance,
but here, on umber earth,
whoever pauses long enough can see
autumn effulgence overflow its swell—
a yellow bird is singing in
a yellow tree.

PROMISING

You promised me you would return,
but you have not returned.

You said returning in the summer would be good
when the round lily pond was filled
with green-framed yellow flowers,
and at the pebble-glinting edge
a bullfrog blinks its golden eyes
to welcome in the sun.

Or maybe umber autumn
equally would satisfy for my return, you said,
with ripeness ripening
and huddled bushes burgeoning
with berries glowing sunrise red.

A good time also to return, you mused
as I can still recall,
winter too is worth renewing
when the elk herd follows its
bare ancestral path
across the crackling ice-fringed stream,
with steps deliberate and sure,
their smoke of breath made visible.

But winter came and winter
is now gone again,
and you have not returned.

Ah! Spring, you cried out, spring
will come, the season of renewal by design—
when all alive things are
intended to return for sure, for sure.

My dreamy thoughts drift off to emptiness,
but I'm determined to remain
to wait for your returning.
Suspended in your absence,
without weather, without scenery, without
blue shadows brooding in the hills,
for the summer, for the winter, for the autumn, for the spring.

PORTRAIT IN DECEMBER LIGHT

"Don't make the visible
easy to see," she said,
in her melodic voice,
posed by the window where
hazy December light
softened her cheek but left
blue shade around one eye,
which looked inwards with my
aroused imagining
to intimate a sense
of obscure origins
that as a slender child
she nearly drowned, but that
her father rescued her.
    And so I painted her far
into my dark, beyond
my father's heart attack,
beyond my grandfather's
escape from Stalingrad,
beyond my ancestor
who broke and sculpted stones
in red Egyptian sun.
    Was this my own lost dream
in which the father there
is me, striding in the foam
among the sandpipers
and windward-whirling gulls?
I asked myself as I,
attempting to compose,
paintbrush in hand, my thoughts,
while finding greens and blues,
purples and reds, their shades
and their elusive tints,
their vibrant inwardness.

"Is this then fatherhood?"
I asked again with her
before me sitting there,
in intermittent light
so near and yet remote,
so vastly far away.

INWARD BLUE

It's midway into March,
and morning mist
darkens the blue haze of the distant
mountain range
so that I find
this darker melancholy blue
expanding in
the skyscape of my mind.
And now noon sun illuminates
snow-covered peaks
with such intensity
I have to close my eyes
so I will not forget
my dwelling on the blue that frames
its jagged silhouette.
Down from the mountain's
crevices and slopes
blue evening shade flows forth
and merges with
the somber purple of my mood
then gathers in a hush of trees
that brood the way their shadows brood.
An unimpeded moon leaps out
above the mountain peak; its glow suffuses
my deep drowsiness which sees
a purple residue of fading light
that savors its blue memories.
Moonlight upon wind-rippled snow
with all its hues of purple shade
reveals a midnight glimmer of
an enticing swoon,
and *oh* and *ooh* and *oooh* and *ah*,
I will myself to disappear
in my own unfathomable blue.

ISHMAEL

My special job that boyhood summer
was to feed the ducks,
keep their pen clean,
prevent the dogs from hassling them.
Sleek, luminescent white,
self-confident and gratified
to have been born as ducks without
to be or not to be uncertainty,
they honked and hooted
when they greeted me
each time the barn door opened,
and I suddenly appeared.
One morning I was taken by surprise
to see piled on a neat nest of straw
six gleaming eggs;
I felt instinctively
that I had been appointed
guardian and caretaker.
I brought the parent ducks
fresh water twice a day
and made sure that the nesting
straw was fresh and dry,
the eggs secure.
One agitated dawn
I went to tend them earlier than usual,
and to my horror all the eggs were
smashed apart
with only fragments of split shells
remaining in their nest—
that is, all eggs but one.
The only egg spared from the
weasel's night attack
was merely slightly cracked.
I tapped it three times with my fingernail,

and, by god, a plump baby duck
popped out.
I did not know back then
"imprinting" was the term for
what occurred,
 but the first moving object
that a hatchling sees
is permanently registered as
MOTHER in its brain,
and that by serendipity was me.
I'm sure you get my point:
fate had decreed that I become
a mother duck.
The duckling, named Ishmael,
faithfully would follow me
along the path that led up to our house
where I would tuck him in the
pocket of my flannel shirt,
his head above the leather rim
so that he could survey the universe,
and I would read to him
in my most lilting cadences
to entertain the both of us.
With summer's end
I put him in the
pond to set him free.
For three whole days,
he circled past
the lily pads, and then
departed—maybe
for a larger pond
where ducks assemble
to relate their
laughing fables of escape.

OPENNESS

With nothing she still wants to call her own
and no one she depends upon,
her distant parents now deceased,
and having grieved quite long enough
and thus now unencumbered
and at ease with emptiness,
she packs her car with camping gear,
a stove, a tent, and launches out
early at hazy dawn
to nowhere in particular.
The flat and flowing road at noon
extends before her dreaming eyes
like someone else's memory
of finally returning home.
The plotted countryside recedes
into long rows of hooded corn
and fields of mottled cows
posed almost motionless
beneath brushed stationary clouds.
She sees a swirl of dusty wind
that looks as if it wants
to take on human form,
but no, the swirl dissolves back
into shapelessness.
To her astonishment,
she is elated by this image
of such airy openness
expressing her elusive mood,
so undefined and tentative.
And soon she will see
gleaming mountain peaks,
and she'll ascend into a forest dense with evergreens
and ghosts of pale, decaying trees,
a waterfall cascading
through its intermittent shade

as silent deer who read the wind
stare silently at her,
whoever she might be.
And soon she will descend
along a sweep of undulating hills
where she will pause to listen
to a yellow-throated meadowlark,
perched on a tumbling cedar fence,
whose lilting notes will welcome
her arrival in the dusk.
She hears, puffed full
with its melodic song,
a glow emerging in the dark,
the trilling voice of her serenity—
the meadowlark.

PRAYER FOR A PAINTED TURTLE

Mid-June, and I was hiking
on a woodland path
about a hundred yards
from a secluded lake
when suddenly I came upon
a turtle digging a round nest
with her hind feet just inches deep
in which she laid six eggs,
in evenly spaced intervals,
as silently I cheered her on.
    I have forgotten what
my destination was that day,
entirely absorbed
while watching her produce
her precious eggs
and cover them with loosened soil,
trusting the earth to hatch them all
in two months of allotted time.
    And as I watched her
I imagined that I well could be
observing her ten million years ago—
about how long her species has survived
without the need for change,
unlike our readapting kind.
    I'm doubtful that I can account
for the elation that I felt,
troubled with apprehension,
on witnessing her feat
of fabulous fecundity.
    Drowsy sun-worshipper,
she'll stretch her limbs out
on a floating log
to help sustain her body's heat.
Her sleek black shell reflects
noon's dazzling blaze

in the reverberating sky
which spreads its luminosity
to summon up an aura
to surround her gleaming head
and brighten her shell's red design,
as if effusively for show,
repeating on its bottom rim.
    So what can I, as bystander,
contribute to this summertime display?
Am I the means by which
unmediated nature
contemplates itself? Or have I
been assigned the role of
guardian?
    If so, how deeply do I need to change,
subdue the instinct to subdue,
to dominate, that turtles
may not lose their place to breed,
their home in our indifferent air,
that they may thrive and flourish
perilously longer in my care?

RABBIT REFLECTION

Brer Rabbit searched the woods to find the place
Where he could pause beside a pond to see
His visage, his own flawless rabbit face,
Unsupervised by the wood's deity.

But a voice called, "You will be punished soon
Before dawn's glimmerings resume their dance,
Transformed into a slack-jawed drooling goon,
Befitting narcissistic arrogance."

His beauty was too potent to resist;
Alas, he peeked again, and he was changed;
This happens when a deity is pissed,
When self-love is distorted and deranged.

It is a tale of warning and of sorrow
That we are hare today and goon tomorrow.

KEEPING TIME

"Devouring time," the Bard declaims—as if
We eat just to be eaten in the end
By patient worms. What greening time can give,
It gives by pausing when our voices blend
Just as a hummingbird suspends midflight.
"Let's meet at noon," you say, "beside the gate."
I watch a luminescent dragonfly alight
On one poised consummately still to mate.
And still time flies when we are having fun.
Take note! We can keep time by keeping time,
When what is past has now again begun,
When what is yours curves back, returns as mine.
Now greeny Kermit blinks his golden eyes,
Proclaims, "Time's fun when you are having flies."

THE RED FOX

I.

The red fox in his den
observes me watching him.
He sniffs the wafting scent
of morning in the air
and wonders whether I
will hunker down or else
pass on, impermanent.

II.

Stiffly, he glares out from
his cradled dark. "Take heed,"
he says. "You will miss me
when I at last begin
being gone. You will have one
less metaphor to declare your wariness,
your stealth, your origin."

III.

"Few creatures in the wild
hang on to old age,"
I tell the fox when we
meet in a silent glade.
"Your pity is misplaced,
old man," he says.
"I do not wish to scowl like you,
even in wrinkling shade."

IV.

The red fox steps into
a clearing in the woods. He says,

"We're not designed to keep
what we need to possess—
together or alone."

V.

The fox's den returns
to being just a hole.
Absence alone is all in
darkening shade. Only
the voiceless dark remains.

TICKLED

It is a mystery that kids enjoy
Being tickled. Soul-shaking laughter is inspired,
And revealed, whether in girl or boy.
A trusted friend or parent is required
To liberate such laughter one can squeeze
Not only from a human child who begs
For more, but also from baby chimpanzees
Or baby gorillas whose arms and legs
Gyrate wildly in an ecstatic swoon,
Whose panting laughter cries out soulfully,
"Please stop, no please continue." So too the moon
draws ancestral tides from the body
Of the salt, everlasting sea to call
The deep-ribbed mystery, "Laughter is all!"

BISON ASCENDING

On a steep hill, almost
motionless, there stands an
old ragged bison with
one glumly broken horn.
His attentive ears twitch;
slant light glints in his eyes.

With a great sudden whoosh,
he sprouts angular wings
that stir a rousing wind
rising in swoops and swirls.

My unencumbered soul
will seek him browsing in
a field of balsamroot
spreading beyond my sight
in humming paradise.

THE RETURN OF THE WOOLY MAMMOTH

Protected behind museum glass
in simulated ice
a wooly mammoth stares at me
and animates my plans.
    I'll call my roommate—
Lord of our Home Terrarium—at the new genome lab
where he's preserved some bone fragments
which contain
some mammoth DNA,
and then we'll smuggle them
to my resourceful brother at the zoo
where he tends the grown elephants.
We will extract rare DNA,
then splice it in the throbbing vein
inside an elephant's thin ear.
    Behold! Two swift years pass,
and I'm the parent of
a pachyderm.
We'll move up to Alaska where
I'll clone another baby mammoth
from the first. And then,
by God, I'll clone myself.
    "Multiply! Multiply!" I will enjoin myself—
creator, creature, both—
each hair upon each head,
numbered and immortalized in
my shaggy doggerel story. Oh!
Genial conception of monumental resurrected forms,
Obliterated by our ancestors,
Fantastical yet true,
I sing this song and celebrate
your late return to welcome you.

STILL HERE

I'm guessing the same tufted bird
is sitting in a patch of snow
on the same branch of the birch tree
I planted twenty years ago.

Nature likes little repetitions,
cyclings, lawful geometry,
alternatives emerging,
and the ripeness of variety.

I'm guessing that same tufted bird,
is an ordinary Western jay,
whose shades of blue erupt
into an orange ray

of intermittent evening light
as if its fresh effulgence meant
something the bird might feel—
perhaps acceptance or content.

I'm guessing that "content" will be
the word repeating in my mind
to keep my shaking steady,
and to help me find

myself again at the beginning,
whose initiating cause
brought forth repeatings
as our everlasting laws.

And so, let me repeat once more
my picture of a bird perched in a tree
before I contemplate where he has gone
dissolving now in memory

before the final silence
and the final guess,
where a solitary bird stands guard
outside the gated emptiness.

REVERSED CLOSURE

Can good will, reason, empathy suffice
For us to crush desire to dominate
Our fellow creatures? With a roll of dice,
Will snake eyes' chance control the fang of fate?
I write of our willful apocalypse.
Although evolved gloom seems impersonal,
Unfathomable mankind sorrow grips
My tightened throat. My gasping heart is full
Of grievances, remorse: our rebel choice
To subdue nature scalds the air, sickens the sea
With radiated whales whose choral voice
Will cease for terminal eternity.
We breed prolific weapons to destroy,
Contending with primal mortality.
As if betrayed, we mourn remembered joy.
And where now is the tangled wilderness?
Where is the sabbath of our fertile time?
We share one creature breath to curse or bless,
And I, Dear Earth, elect to leave you with a rhyme.

DINOSAUR DIALOGUE

Still half asleep, he bolts up stiff in bed,
and cries out, "Oh, the dinosaurs are dead,
I see their final footsteps in the sand,
I hear the thud of their tremendous weight
as they collapse and shudder and go still."

She pulls the covers to her chin, replies,
"Yes, dear, word's out—most people are aware
an asteroid crashed down in Mexico
and blasted up the suffocating dust,
obstructing the choked sun and killing plants
that dinosaurs depended on, killing
the dinosaurs that fed on dinosaurs.
But that occurred millennia ago;
the time to grieve has passed. Go back to sleep!"

"Maybe," he says, "in some forgotten place
a few have managed to survive, and we
can put them into zoos where they would be
protected and secure, each one content,
and we—we could watch over them,
and spend our breezy summer afternoons,
observing how they entertain themselves
and amble through the unaccounted days."

"Lie down, dear," she replies, "they are all gone.
They had their time—much longer than we have—
be comforted, their doom made possible
that cringing little mammals would emerge
from their cold caves into the blaze of day,
grow murderously smart and multiply,
and now too many of us clog the earth,

but who would wish to see us blotted out?
Not me, not this contender with the night!
Just yesterday, no doubt by chance,
I saw a cuddly brontosaurus at the store
on closeout sale, and guess what happened, dear.
Since dinosaurs are hard to find these days,
I bought it right there bingo! on the spot
to celebrate our anniversary."

CALL OF THE LAKE

Can human love contend with emptiness
below, around, above, beyond?
Thick smoky mist arises from the lake;
a few dry leaves cling to a poplar tree.
Raised up on the shore's edge,
a cedar house with a wide lookout deck
stands with its door ajar,
thumping in the intermittent wind.
Last summer on a moonlit night
the owners drowned—
an accident, though some suppose
it was a double suicide.
Their children claimed their parents seemed content.
Both were historians,
recording conflagrations of desire,
uprisings, circumstantial violence,
always with variations, always the same,
with respite only long enough to dream of peace.
But it is possible their father
had a terminal disease
and that the two decided they would die
together in the soft embrace
of their ancestral element.
And, after all, a body is composed
primarily of water, like the lake.
Thick mist arises from the ghostly lake.
A few dry leaves cling to a poplar tree
where an indistinguishable bird alights.
Can human love contend with emptiness,
with emptiness, with emptiness?

DISGUISE

Just four years old, our daughter
liked her angel costume best
with shiny feathered wings
that tightly fit her slender arms.
She had a wooden wand
with an illuminated star
at its spellbinding tip
that granted wishes
as she thought of them.

Excited, she would flap her wings
and do a wiggly dance
in cadence with imaginary flight.
She made her Halloween debut
oblivious of late October's frosty wind,
her candy basket swinging in her hand,
soon to be rewarded to the brim.
Her older brother had a vampire mask
with yellowish protruding fangs
and bloody drippings down its jaw.
His gloves had long, curled nails
to match the lizard green of his felt cape;
to his particular delight,
his sneakers had been dyed
the same shade of foreboding green.

Kids like to be concealed at play,
yet recognizable to those
who care for them.
And maybe it's the same with us adults
except that we prefer the line between disguise
and recognition to be blurred—
to cast a shadow of uncertainty
when we fear being understood.

My wife's plan was to go
as Cleopatra in a linen dress
with a bejeweled neckband
and a silk multicolored sash
around her waist that flowed down
to the ground along her thigh.
And she would flash a silver bracelet
on one wrist and wear another made of gold
that curled around her arm and showed a snake head
slightly lifted at the circle's end.
Her eyes would be
outlined in charcoal black,
a touch of glitter on her sandaled feet.
The role assigned to me
was to remain at home
and hand out chocolate kisses
to all trick-or-treaters
crowded in our entryway.
I wore a jacket and a tie
in order to convey
a sense of my authority
to exercise control
with so much sweet indulgence
tempting them to craziness.
I felt depleted following the
frenzy at my door;
it seemed to me that suddenly
the hour had gotten late.
No one remained, but a full moon
emerged out from behind a cloud
as stillness shuddered in the empty street.

An isolated figure
in a grinning, white-cheeked mask
approached me, step by measured step,
concealed in a black overcoat,
then paused there for a moment

as a last few leaves
descended from a maple tree.
The grinning shape grasped
both edges of the overcoat
and flung it open in one swoop,
and there a flawless woman stood
completely naked
in the moonlight radiance.
I staggered back into the house—
could that white phantom be my wife?
but she—she vanished down the street
as silently the swirling cloud
obscured the moon.

After my wife returned
and put the clinging kids to bed,
I sat her down and told her
what incredibly occurred
at our own home that night,
and she replied,
"I wonder who the woman
might have been."
And now nobody seems the
same to me.

PAPAGENO REPLAYED

In Mozart's opera *The Magic Flute*,
The keyed-up lovers, high and low, dispute

Their mortal fate with their immortal art
As Papageno's wish defines his part:

His glockenspieler's role in fleeting life:
To find and woo and win a pretty wife

By showing stamina and self-control
In his bird-catcher's lusty earth-bound role.

He closed his eyes, poured out his trilling heart,
Trusting his glockenspieler's soaring art,

But when he opened them—must age be told—
Before him sat a crone eighty years old.

His guiding spirits had contrived to best
Make urgent his heart's fortifying test:

To see if he truly was worthy of
The cornucopia of wedded love.

He cursed his loneliness and wailed, "Nicht gut,
Das glockenspiel ist ja kaput."

(The opera is German; thus, it's right
To praise its rapture of gemütlichkeit.)

So hopelessly he wandered on his way
Through joyless night and melancholy day,

But soon he paused and said, "I'll count to three,
Then hang myself upon this willow tree."

At once his supervising spirits sighed,
"Do not forsake your magic bells," they cried:

"We know how disillusioned humans feel,
But you can trust your chiming glockenspiel."

So Papageno played again and "Ah!"
Before him posed pretty Papagena

Who greeted him with hands on hips
And his resounding name upon her lips.

Take note, you lovers, let your words take wing,
Let Mozart sing for you, let Mozart sing.

And may your wooing rise out of its swoon,
And your good glockenspiel remain in tune

So that your progeny proliferate
From warbling wilderness to sunlight's gate.

FOREVER

Who could have thought eternity would be so brief?
There's barely time for us to say farewell.
The willow mourns its final fallen leaf.
The tolling bell tolls for a tolling bell.

My body tired when I last urged it on.
I have outlived my immortality.
New swans are here; the swans I fed are gone.
Renewal breeds the gloom of memory,

Of bygone happiness, no more, no more,
Shared peaches dripping bite for luscious bite.
No genie bottle swirled up on the shore.
No more your face by day, your arms by night.

Eternity forever vanishing
Is the immortal song we mortals sing.

DOUBLING DOWN

I.

In an earlier life
I was an elephant.
Born from an ovum and
Elephant sperm.

Now just my name remains,
Genealogically,
Truncated playfully:
Bob-Pachyderm.

II.

Writing a poem, you should
Stop at the end, although
You've let a genie out
Of its bottle.

Humpty tells Alice that,
Hermeneutically,
If she doubts him, just ask
Aristotle.

III.

How to commemorate
Jurassic plenitude?
Choose pterodactyl as
Example one.

Look at his crooked wings
Ornithologically,
Praise him dactylically,
If just for fun.

IV.
Darwin thinks earthworms are
Nature's first gardeners,
Foraging through the dark,
Safe underground.

O brave progenitors,
Hermaphoditical,
Adam and Eve in one,
Let praise resound!

V.
In the bleak beginning
A lone prokaryote
Bonds with a cellmate to
Change "I" to "Us."

Thanks, Nature, for spawning
Connubiality,
Easing gloom by sharing
A nucleus.

VI.
Given sufficient time,
Nim Chimpsky can, by chance,
Type out Shakespeare's Hamlet,
Perhaps absurd.

But he may think it's his
Autobiography,
Or just that he likes to
Monkey with words.

VII.
To cure mortality,
The ache of finitude,
Drink from the Holy Grail;
Let there be hope!

To cure the common cold,
Neurotic misery,
Unenebriated,
Try chicken soup!

VIII.
Have you no Jewish jokes,
Bernie, you kvetcher, to
Keep your brash pandering
Locked in its box?

Sanctimoniously,
Your spiels are red herrings,
Not enough bagels and
Not enough lox.

IX.
Nature's mutations, like
Slips of the tongue, bought forth
The duck-billed platypus.
In a rare mood,

Our quacky mayor claimed
Egomaniacally,
He raised our town to a
new platitude.

X.
Rewriting Truman's boast
That the buck stops with me,
President Kennedy,
Now it is clear,

Told his Secret Service that,
Conspiratorial,
My Monroe Doctrine is:
Buxom stops here.

XI.
Einstein, God does play dice.
Anyone twice divorced
Know passion's energy
Is swiftly spent.

Bohred by uncertainty,
Walking time's plank you trust
$E=MC^2$
Is permanent.

XII.
If gravity is strong
Enough, space will collapse
To a prodigious and
Terminal crunch.

Theologically,
I'd like to witness this
Concluding spectacle.
I'll bring my lunch.

CONQUEROR

Let me assure you would-be fathers
nothing has been embellished here meant to
discourage you. I am just hoping to achieve perspective
in recalling my own history better to understand
our country's furious disputes.
My father was a New Deal Democrat,
a senator from our home district
in the ethnic territory of the Bronx.
A gentle man with gentle friends,
he was respected and admired
across the cultural divides.
One day—the origin, as I assume,
of my political anxieties—
his colleague, Justice Joseph Cohn,
remembered only as the father of
notorious Roy Cohn, arrived at our house in
order to review some legal documents,
and, fatefully, he brought his son with him.

Roy Cohn, despite his father's good-willed generosity,
became the eager acolyte
of mentor Joe McCarthy, scourge
and chief tormentor of suspected Communists,
even their sympathizers and apologists.
I was contentedly constructing an aspiring
tower in my sandbox
in our fenced-in backyard
when the two fathers led Roy out
to play with me, and who,
O goddess of contingency,
can fathom what dispute occurred that star-crossed day?

So up I rose to my full four-year height
and conked him soundly on the head

with my red shovel in the heat
of wrathful righteousness.
It must have been a mighty conk because
I think they took him to the hospital,
and I, it is my destiny to say,
will never know if I'm, in fact, the cause
of his unbounded hatred
of suspected enemies
and all the suffering that he
inflicted on the innocent.
McCarthy's sly, conspiratorial beliefs
degraded public discourse, poisoning
the common well of tolerance.
I still can picture those inquisitors,
as if their sweating heads
had merged upon a single neck,
as they bent right above
the blaring microphone
while sentencing good citizens
to shame and banishment.

So you can understand what troubles me
in these accusatory times.
Without my blow, might Roy
have turned out even worse, a murderer, a terrorist?
Or, had I conked him even harder
when his father thrust him in my sovereign domain,
could the Homeric blow I smote
have rearranged his tangled brain
and redirected his instinctual malevolence?

Alas, my days of conking are long gone,
though that may well be for the best,
yet I still wonder if
there's something left for me to do to ease
our ravaged country's agony.
And now I see myself like Hector standing

on the sandy shore of windblown Ilium,
hoping my South Bronx story will be told
to entertain you worried fathers anywhere
that you are willing to risk raising sons.

THE DOOR

My long-time friend was a philosopher.
He placed his faith—pardon the paradox—
in reason, logical analysis,
deduction (keeping one's ducks in a row).
He loved his family, his St. Bernard.
He liked canoeing, skiing, birdwatching—
"Outdoor Highs," he called them. He sought for grace
in works of self-transcending intellect,
like Plato's dialogues of ideal forms
and mazes of loquacious Socrates.
And, only certain of uncertainty,
"Agnostic "was the philosophic term by which
he chose to designate himself.

His wife was brought up in the Church, and though
she knew the arguments for doubt,
she held to her beliefs—the reach of hope,
the consolation of an afterlife.
When he was lying in the hospital,
unconscious at the end, she held his hand,
keeping vigil for his last days as she
recounted to me almost in a trance.
Then, suddenly, he lifted up his head,
opened his eyes, and in a rising voice
proclaimed, "A door! I see a door!" And then
his breathing softened and his hand let go.

I was away, on one of my retreats,
and when I met her later following the busy funeral,
she still appeared strangely disembodied and remote,
but wanted to explain the door. "The door,"
she said, "must mean that he is telling me
there is an entrance to another world;
I should be comforted and reassured
that we'll be reunited where losses

are restored beyond imagining,
though maybe marriage has not
been designed for inexhaustible eternity.

   I did not say so at the time, but I
don't think that we can know our species' fate
or how the universe will terminate,
collapse on its own self or just thin out
expanding into empty nothingness,
but I'm damn certain there's no evidence,
none, for an afterlife or for a god
who suffers for our human suffering.
I have no hopes beyond this mortal world,
feel free to label me an "Atheist."
Although when I'm way out there at the edge,
I can imagine Yahweh, having tried,
but failed, to teach us humans holiness,
decides to try another strategy
to simplify fruitful engendering,
so women can feel free and self-composed,
self-serving, self-entertaining. Is this
perplexing and ambiguous? For sure,
vexed Yahweh rules the heavens and the earth
forever with a rod of irony.

   The night after his wife and I conversed,
I had a puzzling, agitating dream.
Don't get me wrong, I don't mean to offend
or be politically incorrect.
One can't be held responsible for what
just pops up in one's mind, like Yahweh when
he's speaking in the voice of Balaam's ass,
(partly for laughs?) or for what one dreams.

   Within my dream, I woke up in my tent
and crawled out wobbly from my sleeping bag
into a clearing in the winter woods.

A light wet snow revealed a brambled trail
with recent ski tracks down the mountainside.
When I reached bottom, the straight trail veered left
into a one-way street where my pale friend,
wearing white gloves, waved the stalled traffic on
as pulsing green light blinked across his face.
The street became a moaning tunnel with
white walls that stretched beyond my squinting sight,
yet seemed somehow to narrow and converge.
I looked again and thought I saw far off
a glowing door. I am nearsighted, so
I couldn't read the sign upon the door.
As I got closer, I could faintly hear
beyond the door the titillating sound
of laughter lilting in the languid air
of paradisal possibility.
"Incredible," I told my waking self.
But, "Ladies Only" was what the sign said.

BELIEVABLE

       I am not sure how many years ago
I read my elegiac poem
at the Moonbeam Society
about a hunting trip
my brother and I took in northern Maine:
an accident occurs
in which I shoot my brother in the head;
he tries to speak some final words,
but I can't understand his gurgling sounds—
forgiveness or perhaps a curse.
All brothers are tormented by
conflicted feelings over time.

I lay him gently in the bow of our canoe
and paddle him down river
to the nearest one-bar town
to have him cremated
and bring his ashes home
in an oak box engraved with flying
birds—an image of migration that
appealed to him.

Right after the
performance of my poems,
a slim, attractive woman walked
hesitantly to the podium
to offer me condolences:
"How can such sorrow be endured
by creatures frail as we humans are?"
she softly asked, but, flustered on the spot,
I felt compelled to say
I had contrived the grim account
of shooting my own brother in the woods.
"I do not have a brother," I declared.

"You mean your poem did not tell the truth,"
she bluntly said and scrutinized my eyes.
"A poem, to be believable," I lectured her,
"requires conviction that it might be true
in someone's actual experience,
and, in that metaphoric sense,
the brother in my poem is more than fictional.
Verisimilitude is what I struggle to achieve."

"You mean you lied to me," she persevered,
and roughly pulled away her hand.
A furtive teardrop glistened on her cheek,
and, angrily, she stomped out of the auditorium.

For days her shaken image troubled me,
and so I asked around until I learned her name, got her address,
and showed up at her home one windy night,
requesting she invite me in
and let me try again to justify myself.
"I told you that I made the poem up
because you seemed so terribly upset,
and I just didn't want to burden you.
or have you question what my
fabricating motive might reveal.
I guessed you must have lost
someone you dearly loved."

"How kind and caring of you," she
replied, and took my hand in both of hers, her bracelets
sliding down and covering her wrists.
"Your guess was right, intuitively right," she said.
"My sister drowned when we were
on vacation in the Keys in Florida.
She got a cramp or maybe
she was dragged down by an undertow,
I couldn't rescue her—
and Oh, how quickly she went down

almost as if she really didn't care.
I never knew what caused her gloom
or kept her mostly to herself."

She paused, drew back, so I
no longer felt her soft breath
touching me,
and then, impatiently, she asked,
"How would you feel if I now told you
that I improvised this story of my sister's death,
that secretly I am a poet too—
yes, isn't everyone?"

That was the very instant
when I fell in love with her—
the instant when
I wished that we could all
acknowledge even our most
innocent mendacities.
Our desperate deflections
are accepted as our own although
unscrupulous necessity demanded
I invent this narrative about the tender lady
who critiqued my poem,
someone who understood me to the core,
someone who still could love me as I am.

ENCIRCLED

   A harvest moon
arises in an azure sky
above the mountain's
glowing silhouette—
a perfect circle in my sight,
inviting me to contemplate
a transcendental form
that Plato must have often seen
above the Parthenon—a form
commencing from a starting point
on its circumference
that might be anywhere
and leading to no necessary end.
And thus the idea of eternity,
returning to what has never gone away,
may well appear as visible
without one's being present
to observe the scene.
   And so I contemplate a form
that is ongoing and without
a stopping point and not requiring
my beholding it aglow
in its blue atmosphere.
"Exactly right," Plato exclaims.
eager as always for some lively dialogue,
as he steps forth between
the columns of the Parthenon.
"The circle concept," he declaims,
"does not need us to perceive
its imitation in this shadow of a world."
   "True also," I chime in, determined
to display how up-to-date my thinking is,
"of our entire universe,
if it turns out to be correct,
that time and space

emerged as one with the Big Bang,
and that expanding space / time,
continues to recede
as far as tugging gravity allows
until all matter comes
accelerating back
to culminate in a Big Crunch.
And then in its inevitable turn,
a new Big Bang explodes,
as if born out of nothingness,
all evidence of its past cycle now erased,
and off life goes again
in a stupendous evolutionary romp
to constitute a circle in the void,
a repetition, a renewal, a return. "

   "Bravo!' Plato paternally applauds,
'I see that you have understood
my concept of abiding essences
and reaffirmed the fellowship
of time-transcending dialogue."

   He tells me, "You'll feel better now that
permanence, platonic forms—excuse me
for indulging in self-reference—
is fundamental in your own philosophy."

   I must admit I was relieved
to have his words of consolation.
"Were I to trust my own experience,
life seems so transient, so ephemeral,
a wisp of breath, a drop of dew,
without a purpose or a goal
or compensation for inevitable loss."

   "Goals are elusive, that's for sure,"
Plato replies, "and death
an interrupted sentence
not to be completed or resumed.
Let me remind you
of my teacher Socrates'

concluding words before
he drank the lethal hemlock down
as Athens' rigid law required,
surrounded by his grieving followers:
   "I need to reimburse Asclepius
for the fine cock I bought from him."
Confused by what appeared to
undermine one's self-absorbed high-mindedness
or to perplex posterity with fears
about the fate of justice in
this insubstantial world
or in a vague, uncertain afterlife,
wanting to remain in harmony
with his ironic, darker side,
   I added, "Well, of course, there is
an alternate scenario in which
the universe goes on expanding,
dissipating all its heat, until
nothing is left but inert entropy
without a circular return
to friends and family
without a moon above the Parthenon,
without a lofty elegy
to mourn our vanishing
or hope new order will emerge."
   "My dear star-struck inheritor,"
Plato opined,
"I ask you to revisit *The Symposium*,
my dialogue in praise of unifying love—
both bodily and of the soul.
its stages, its distractions, its varieties,
in which frail Socrates, after a long
and raunchy night of drunken talk
with doomed and smitten Alcibiades
and diverse revelers,
is the lone character who still remains
awake, prepared to discourse on

those everlasting themes
of comedy and tragedy,
of self-deception and of penitence,
each necessary in its time and place,
each quickening the other's relevance.
    So come with me, aspiring partner
in conviviality, let's take a stroll
and watch what one might call
the rosy-fingered dawn illuminate
the vaulting columns of the Parthenon.
It's harvest time come round again,
and squabbling citizens
will soon be gathered in the marketplace."

COLORING

Life is a waterfall,
time is a dragonfly,
and colors mean what I
intend them to mean.
Soon in high wakefulness
I will compose a white
epithalamium.
Let passion be violet,
let slumber be blue.
As bleak November nears,
let memory be indigo,
let hope be green.

CHICKEN SOUP

When still at college, living in New York,
away from home, uncertain
what profession I should choose,
without purpose or a cause,
I frequented a cozy Jewish restaurant.
An aged waiter with luminous hair
would greet me by announcing the day's special,
and when I'd say, "Sounds good to me,"
he would reply, waving his pen
like a magician's wand,
"Today you'll have . . ." and,
mocking a stern look,
he would select an alternate,
as if he saw something unique in me.
His choice on my behalf was always to my taste,
what I might have selected for myself,
and he would add, "Fear not,
I won't forget the chicken soup."
And sometimes he would close his eyes and say,
"It's known to cure the common cold,
but also it alleviates
depression and enhances empathy.
It can attune one to
the swirling music of the spheres."
And then he'd throw his head
Back, and he'd laugh.
One day at the semester's end
he simply disappeared,
and when I questioned the gruff manager,
he grumbled, "How should I know
where the old man has gone?"
With him not there for company,
my meal seemed bland and sorrowful.
I tried to track him down
but only found his neighbor,

with her arms protected by a woven shawl,
on a dark street near a bridge.
She told me he had left
no forwarding address.
Perhaps, he had returned to Israel,
as she recalled his words,
"Land of ripe olive groves and dates,
of pomegranates and of oranges,
Land of the Patriarchs, bright land
of the everlasting Book."
She asked me to remain a while
for a hot biscuit and some honeyed tea.

      A decade passed before
I went back to the restaurant
one gray, leaf-curling, misty fall.
Under new management,
it was completely changed:
New paneling, new checkered tablecloths,
and yet, somehow, it seemed the same to me.
I was heartily greeted by a youthful waiter,
just returned from legendary Israel.
He looked at me as if we'd met before,
and, thumbs up, praised the variety
of pizzas, burgers, sandwiches—
"Food for any appetite terrestrial," he said,
"but for those still hungering for
something transcendental," he recommended,
"Nectar and Ambrosia, served on Saturdays
until three stars have risen in the sky."

      "Don't you serve chicken soup?"
I questioned him, incredulous.
"Nutritious elixir, divinity incarnate,
sublimity mundane," I chanted.
To which he added, "and the
ordinary made mightily magnificent!"
his words harmonizing with my own.
I laughed as if my life depended

on this blessed overflow.
"My father used to laugh like that,"
was his spontaneous response.
"I'd recognize that laughter anywhere."

OTHER

And, sometimes, I'm not certain who I am.
Someone to pair with as soon pairs with late,
by moon a tiger, and by sun a lamb,
slow when I hurry, fast to hesitate.
We're first partners in possibility,
and our conclusions are wholly a guess.
I think of you still thinking just of me.
My mind moves forward in its inwardness.
Were you my mother in another life?
Perhaps my sister or my child;
maybe an early lover, or a later wife?
Is that shadow yours by the apple tree?
Meet me a dawn beside the western gate
where leaping streams unwind and merge. I'll wait.

REACHING OUT

What can we beam out from the earth
to some far distant galaxy
to boast of what we are at best
and let new cosmic fellowship begin
across the gulf of space and time?
Would Shakespeare's play King Lear appall
with its dumbfounding cruelty,
children's ingratitude, sadistic hate,
brother betraying his own brother's trust,
or would his empathetic artistry, its measured cadences,
its steady reassuring flow
delight, renew, and offer them
an out-of-world experience
that is uncannily consoling and inscrutably sublime?

RETURNING

      With summer well upon its way,
we started from Long Island Sound
in Roger's sailing skiff, our plan
to circle Martha's Vineyard and return
in time to earn some needed cash
to help pay for tuition in the fall
by pitching bales of harvest hay.
      We both had ended our relationships
for reasons we could not explain—
with girls we thought we'd always love, and so
we needed some adventure
to assuage our restlessness.
      The first day out we ran into a squall
and had to dock in someone's private cove,
where we were threatened by the owner
with a charge of trespassing.
Incredibly, he flashed a gun.
And, panicked, lacking stomach
to dispute his charge,
we scrambled from the quaking dock.
So what in hell, we wondered,
might that enraged man possibly
be hiding there—cocaine, a mistress,
or illegal armaments?
      The second day was beautiful—
just enough breeze to make the sailing smooth,
the slap of waves against the hull hypnotic, musical,
when an enormous motor boat
sped by, deliberately close,
its wake almost capsizing us.
From its plush cabin, people waved
in greeting or in mockery—
how could we know? Not far ahead
we came upon a baseball cap
that nodded gravely with the tide; it fitted when I tried it on.

On the third legendary day,
we woke up early to survey the dawn,
the orange light reflected in
fine crests of foam, the mist
with its own throbbing radiance.
Roger steered from the stern,
and I perched in the bow
to watch for unknown obstacles, debris,
or who knows what the sea cast up.
        And then, as if bone-chilling terror, destined
by the stars, was inescapable,
primeval danger showed itself—
a surge of shark fins headed toward me
slicing smoothly through their element.
I grabbed an oar to fend them off, but then
unfathomable nature intervened,
and the pursuing sharks were instantly
transformed into a dolphin pod
as one by one, spaced evenly,
they dove beneath our heaving skiff
and surged up bubbling on the
other side with whistles,
tweetings, titillating trills.
        Now deep in desolate old age,
my country torn perhaps beyond repair,
beyond redemptive healing or regret,
with hatred breeding hatred in our hearts,
cavorting dolphins leap into my mind;
I see them all returning as their snouts
soar gleaming through the pouring spray—
a swell of choiring in the misty air.
All one—we are all one together there.

OWL IN MOONLIGHT

The snowy owl stares from a hemlock tree.
Blue shadows stretch out in the hazy dawn.
I gaze at you, and you gaze back at me.
The moon seems like the phantom of a form.

The broad-winged owl floats out across a field.
Nothing is changed—nothing remains the same.
Only the changing sameness is revealed
With no indifferent deity to blame.

The owl grabs a warm vole beneath the snow.
A little swelling spot of blood appears
Within the silent moonlight's spectral glow,
And we obey the spell of blurring years.

I gaze at you, and you gaze back at me;
The snowy owl stares from a hemlock tree.

BRAVA

In 1954 the Met staged
a performance of
Guiseppe Verdi's *Il Trovatore*,
his drama of misplaced revenge,
confused identities,
with an extraordinary cast,
including the divine soprano, Zinka Milanov.

This morning I just listened on the air
to Verdi's opera of loss,
taken from the Met's archived collection,
going back almost a century.
And as I listened, suddenly,
across forgotten years, their silences,
I vividly remembered that I actually was there.
Each aria, duet, ensemble,
was rewarded with applause.
In Milanov's climactic aria,
her soft notes were as delicate as dew,
her phrasing smoother than a cherub's cheek.
The audience erupted with renewed applause
that seemed it would outlast eternity.
And then, above the clamor,
"Brava!" cried a voice—
distinct, identifiable.
It was my voice that soared above the cheers,
that voice was mine!

And when, Madama Milinov,
you're chosen by Apollo
to perform for the Society of Verdi Worshippers
in the Olympic theater in the sky,
perhaps you'll recognize my "Brava" there
in the enraptured audience.

But here, right now, in my Montana home,
within the silent shadow of the Mission mountain range,
mist rises from the ice-fringed lake,
in ghostly flickerings and swirls.
A first fine flake of snow,
a perfect hexagon,
floats in mid-air, descends,
and melts in my warm, outstretched palm.
An interweaving wind—as if inspired by Euterpe,
the muse of memory and song—
makes immemorial music
among resonating pines,
true amid brittle tamaracks
in measured intervals,
and quickens to a chorus of concatenated aspen leaves.

"Brava!" I cried. "Bravissima!"

QUAKING ASPENS

I'm thinking of you as you were
that summer by the lake
while watching autumn aspen leaves
quake in the wind
as if they are determined
to maintain their named identity
in bold defiance of their change
to dusty brown, still clinging
to a branch, still holding on.
My gloom needs these brown leaves
to keep you undiminished
in my thoughts—an image
starkly visible to fix upon
and hold indelibly in mind.
I shudder in behalf of everything
that clings to life, holds on
as quaking aspen leaves hold on
contending with the wind, the rain,
the cold encroachment of the night.
My sympathy for all leaves
clinging everywhere tempts me away
from dwelling on your face,
your waving from the autumn lake,
your words absorbed in
rippling water sounds,
as my confusion makes
my gloom still gloomier.
And once again I hear
low echoes of your voice
in wailing of the melancholy loons
that disappeared at summer's end;
I hear the echoes float beyond
the smoke ascending from the chimney stones.
And once again I look for solace
in the quaking leaves

still clinging there, still holding on
with just a slender stem.
Although their green is gone,
they are still there, still quaking
in undiscriminating wind.
Listen, I tell myself, they are
repeating their same brittle sound
as I repeat their brittle sound
the name of quaking aspens makes.
The dusty leaves hold on,
and I maintain my vigil
of their one by one declining number
on the pallid branches in the wind
as I'm attempting to distinguish
each sole rocking leaf as it descends
as if to see your face alone
among the passing faces
that, half recognized, float by
illuminated by the slanting light.
But you are lost amid the multitudes—
your dwindling voice
now indistinguishable from the rest,
as season after season merges
with the one that follows next
and next is followed in its turn.
And who is that now waving from the lake?
Have the familiar loons returned
or are they echoes of past
lingering of lingerings,
that hold on as the quaking leaves hold on,
but only in the mist of memory?

OTTER AT MERIDIAN

He's about eight, she's about four
and they are sitting on a sloping bank
beside a swirling river in abundant May.
They're eating lunch of jelly sandwiches
with thermoses of orange juice
that Mom prepared for them
with candy bars that must be saved until the end.

A sudden swoosh upstream
and down the bank through parting shrubbery
an otter, luminescent in the sun,
swoops down into the current flow
above smooth green and purple stones.
The children jump up to their feet
as lunch boxes fly from their laps
and tumble down into the swirl.

That night at dinner,
they tell their story, how he posed in front of them
and disappeared into the bubbling depths.
But brother drowns his sister out
and she begins to cry.
Mom pats her then lights the candelabra Grandma left behind
whose trembling light suffuses the dim room.
"Otters like being what they are," says Mom.
Dad says, "Otters enjoy both vanishing and reappearing once again."

That happy day a life ago
an otter with his flashing head and gleaming eyes,
halted a moment on a muddy riverbank,
in the approving sun and yet it carried happiness away—
away beyond cascading meteors,
beyond Andromeda,
beyond the border of the Firmament.

WYATT EARP IN PRAISE OF FRIENDSHIP

I drove to Tombstone, Arizona,
To revisit the old cemetery where
Young gunslingers' untended graves
Are now remembered only with their dates.
And then I had a few beers at the bar—
It's called The Crystal Palace to this day—
That Wyatt Earp frequented in his time.
I summoned him like Hamlet's father's ghost.
        The only loyal person in the play
Is Hamlet's school-time friend Horatio
Who suffered lonely Hamlet's suffering
And would have died as one with him except
That Hamlet needed him to live
And chronicle to the unknowing world
The hidden story of Prince Hamlet's life.
        I conjured Wyatt sitting by me there
And asked him if he mainly wished to be
Remembered for winning the great fight
At the OK Corral against all odds.
"No," he replied, " when my story is told,
I want to be recalled forever for
My steadfast friendship with Doc Holliday.
He drank way too much and gambled,
Yet he was there when I most needed him
With nothing measurable to be gained
The day we fought the Clantons to the death
In the notorious OK Corral.
Friendship can free us from the prison of
Just merely being who we are."
        "Wise Aristotle said that without friends
One's life is no more than a dusty wind,
And birth is painfully experienced
As banishment, and death—death comes too soon
The brute body's abandoning the soul."

I asked Wyatt what example he would choose
Of mutual identity in friends
Who despite differences, felt the same pain
That the other felt and shared the other's fate.
"Achilles and Patroclus," Wyatt said;
"When Patroclus put on the armour of
Enraged Achilles, he died his friend's death,
Yet gave him a brief interval in which
To contemplate the vanity of fame.
This was his unexpected victory."

     Emboldened, I inquired, "Who do you think
Might represent the gentler side— the side
Of willing sacrifice that can enlarge
The possibilities of what one is
And what then one is able to achieve?"

     Wyatt replied, "There are no friendship vows
That can surpass in simple eloquence
The words of homesick Ruth to Naomi,
'Wherever you will go, I will go, too,
Your home will be my home, your God,my God.'"

     "My pal Doc Holliday expressed himself
In grunts and groans, but what he
Could not put in words, he did for me.
With him, articulating tenderness
Would be no different from pulling teeth."

     I said, "Now give me an example of
A pair that seems unsuited to be matched,
A taboo pair that crosses boundaries."

     "Okay," said Wyatt as his finger twitched around his glass.
"Beneath a hazy sky on their log raft,"
Said Wyatt as if in a trance,
"Drift Huckleberry Finn and his friend Jim
Bonded in their heart's blood as runaways,
As the roiled Mississippi rose to be
The spirit of their wide-eyed wandering.
Along the sloshing shore, the windy trees
Pointed at their passing, cheering them on.

Their kindness toward each other was so deep,
And so instinctive, it glowed visible
Only at the far reach of consciousness
As when Huck set out for the wilderness,
Or like your imagining yourself right here
Beside me in this echoing saloon,
Not far from Boot Hill Cemetery."
      That's where, dear reader, in my mind,
So many disbelieving gunfighters
Lie there still in the untold legends of
Their interrupted lives, unmourned by friends,
While I retell the fabulous and immemorial
Adventures of gunslinger Wyatt Earp
And his intrepid friend Doc Holliday.

ARIA

What's there? O what remains
that's worth remembering?
I reach my hand out in the dark—
no one is there. I call—
no one is listening.
   A coyote howls at the unveiling moon.
In flute arpeggios, a stream
cascades across protruding stones.
I can smell lilacs after April rain;
I hear whoop of sandhill cranes at dawn.
   Beyond the snow-capped mountain range,
the fresh sun quickens;
 I can discern columns of families,
marching neatly arm-in-arm,
their headphones glistening,
along the heaving road
into the Western haze.
They disappear at the horizon's edge.
My head is tuned to hear the marching beat;
my fingers strum the pulsing intervals.

   An avalanche obliterates itself.
An owl bursts forth from a hushed hemlock tree.
He streaks across the Zodiac
to where my grandfather
lights a thick candle
to begin the holidays.
He can remember his own grandfather,
his shaded brick house
in the village square.
   I see the open upstairs' window,
and hear a piano's resonating notes
as they accompany a musky female voice,
sorrowful and voluptuous,
singing a melody I can recall.

She sings, "Erquicket, erquicket mein Herz."
"Erquicket mein Herz" is what the woman sings
across the windy drift
of the uncertain centuries.

GRANDMA IN LIMBO

I still can see her standing by her sink,
in her pouched apron with its pocket full,
tenderly patting each large matzo ball
into a golden, gleaming perfect sphere.
    She looked directly at me, and she said,
"The Lord designed the world in circles so
each one of us would be included here,
and feel at home. That's why He put the sun
right there for all our eyes to feast upon,
for everyone to look and see the swallows
swoop and swirl and flutter in the sky.
And that is why I make my matzo balls
round as I can to offer God my thanks."
    Then Grandma paused and reached into her pouch,
removed a purple kerchief which she set
upon her head and tied the twisted ends
securely underneath her fleshy chin.
    Her soft voice sounded distant as if she
were in a trance. She said, "The Cossacks came
down howling from the hills
and set ablaze the white wooden schoolhouse.
I hear the horses kicking our barn door
and whinny wildly in the night.
The Cossacks murdered, and they robbed, yet God did nothing
to protect the innocent.
He looked on yet He did not intervene.
But who am I—I just make matzo balls—
to question what God's plans and reasons are?"
    "Your mother was just two years old when we escaped from
Russia in a borrowed carriage,
fleeing at midnight with our bags, fearing
the inevitable next pogrom,
across the European continent.
We bribed our way onto a ship to sail
to a new home here in America

where Grandpa opened up a restaurant.
I did the cooking, and he welcomed all
the Yiddish speaking, laughing customers."

    Her words caught in her throat. She looked away
beyond the dusky rain-streaked window where
I could not follow her. I'm thinking now
I should love all the lost, the innocent,
the way I loved my Grandmother back then,
yes, everyone, beneath the moon, beneath
the stars, beneath the circle of the sun.

LAMENT OF THE LONE RANGER

I've had my second vaccine shot;
the President has said it is okay
to go outside without a mask,
a bachelor, unbridled, free
to whoop it up and horse around.
    But here is my profound dilemma:
when I remove my mask, no one can tell me
who I am; I could be anyone.
    When I confront a robber in the act,
he says, "So who are you to issue an arrest?"
When I prevent a rustler from
stealing some other rancher's cows,
he asks, "What poacher are you working for?"
    Tonto tells me " Kemosabe is
a condescending racist word,
that's got to be eliminated now
with other ethnic references."
    Silver tells me he wants to be known
by the content of his character,
not his color, that the Overture
to Giacomo Rossini's "William Tell"
(who is Italian like Columbus)
which has the rhythm of his galloping,
has surely got to be replaced
with something up-to-date and edgier,
like rap-beat Hamilton,
the hoofer Broadway musical.
    I am not who I am, so should you ask,
1'll tell you that the face-off showdown comes-
as in any wild-west feature film-
when the outlaw virus meets his match
as I put on my own identifying mask.

BLIND

This dark, like drowning, doth more dark beget,
More deeper dark without an orange dawn,
Without a mountain's silver silhouette,
Just hopefulness impotent to be born.
This is the gesture that's without reply,
The aftermath without an origin.
A gaping mouth cries out a silent cry,
An overture unable to begin.
The sea within itself, the inner sea,
Oh what can it remember, what forget?
Can water dream itself as memory?
Can consolation quicken from regret?
I hear the sea—its single syllable:
Original oblivion is full.

SYMMETRY

"The universe is the ultimate free lunch,"
Said Alan Guth; it did not have to be.
Big Bang will culminate in a big crunch—
What experts call a singularity,

If there is mass and gravity enough
To bring this vast explosion hurtling back—
Counting neutrinos, all the spooky stuff,
Dark matter and dark energy—to black

Alpha originating, nothingness.
A new big bang will usher forth and be
Creator once again of time and space.
This is the same immortal symmetry

The visionary poet William Blake
Saw as a tiger burning in the night
As a design a deity would make
Of fear transmogrified into delight.

At once, last becomes first, first becomes last.
To be is nothing, nothing is to be.
The future is as fated as the past.
The moment now contains eternity.

I think of the designer, his design,
Till thought collapses on itself and then
A wish is all that's left of me still mine:
I wish to see my mother once again.

MARRIED

I.

Friends tell him that he has a pleasing smile,
except when his lip presses back too hard,
revealing his incisors as too large,
protruding in the mellow northern light.
His wife has a recurring dream
in which she is a young girl once again
painting the slatted picket fence in front
across the lawn a luminescent white
except for the far picket on the left,
and the far picket on the right
which she covers with two thick coats of black.
"Didn't your mother warn you," he remarks,
"about Jewish vampires who are able to
disguise themselves as lawyers, doctors, or
like me, even as cosmologists?"

"Stargazing husband and true soul mate of
my wildest fantasies," she then replies,
with fingertips together in prayer,
"You're free to kiss me anywhere you like,
even on the pulsing blue vein on my neck.
Sometimes at night before I fall asleep,
I think of home, the farm, the animals.
I miss my billy goat. It was my job
to comb his beard, to feed and water him.
Let's visit when the holidays come round.
I'll bring my dad your latest article
about dark matter and dark energy."

II.

He wonders if she wonders why
she made the choice to marry him.
Beneath each motive, he believes,
there lies another deeper still
and yet another further down
to an unfathomable depth.

And all we can be certain of
is that we do not know what we
don't know, its fatal consequence.
Perhaps our solitary choice
is to accept necessity,
the gravity of consciousness.
          A giant pelvic bone pokes out
from loosened mountain sediment.
A black hole gobbles up a star.
In only fifteen billion years
our sun will crunch down on itself,
explode and thus exterminate
the planets in its influence.
All we can do is shudder and
bear witness mutely in the mind.
          We did not choose to have free will.
What message shall we beam out to
an unattended universe?
O, Alpha Centauri, neighbor,
is anybody listening?
Does anyone speak Yiddish there?

                    III.
          Thanksgiving day, and they arrive at dusk.
There is the picket fence—her parents still
are living there. The sculpted iron gate
has three sleek ravens perched on it as if
to welcome them. They lift their heads and call,
then flap off crying in the fellow dark.
A cobbled path leads to the entryway
where from the eave a row of icicles
glistens in the diminished evening light.
Her mother greets them at the door. She is
attractive, he thinks, and he
can see her daughter's mischief in her face.
Her father has a patch on his right eye,
and drops his cane when he embraces her.
          They sit around the fire and reminisce—

how premature she came into the world,
and how their neighbor's house burned down that night.
"We think the time has come to sell the house
and move into town," her mother says again.
"The main branch of the maple out in front
broke off last summer in a thunderstorm.
Perhaps you noticed when you first arrived."

   "Let's go back to the barn to see my goat,"
she says. "I'm sure that he remembers me."

   The aged goat paws the fresh straw and then
greets her, pressing his cheek against her cheek
as she bends forward in complete response.
"My God!" she cries, "The goat resembles you—
his beard, his weary-eyed, Talmudic stare,
the toothy, confident, determined jaw.
Strange that I never noticed this before."

   Let's walk back to the stream and cross the bridge
my father built of fitted maple planks
to where he made a clearing in the woods
in which to rest his treasured telescope.
A troll moved in beneath the arching bridge
according to her father's diary.
Where he suspects it was a Jewish troll
that made its home in his ancestral woods."

   In silence, hand-in-hand, they dally there
together gazing at the pulsing stars.
They see glittering Orion, Taurus,
the mighty bull, and Scorpio the crab,
and there the overflowing dipper with
its sturdy handle, pointing to the north,
as guide for amateur adventurers.
And south, above the deep horizon's rim
strides bright, surefooted Capricorn, the goat,
her husband's astral representative.
Implacable realist, he know that
compatible marriage depends on chance
or fate—celestial configurings—
or only ordinary mazel tov.

MY DECLARATION OF DEPENDENCE

Without a god who fashions us in his/
her image, there could never be human
equality and universal rights.
But, truth to tell, the evidence is that (read Darwin)
we are different in strength,
in talent, temperament, intelligence,
grace to cooperate. Some are just bad:
greedy, deceitful, selfish, murderous.
And cultures, too, societies, and nations
all have vastly varied governments
and divergent fates. Some win in gory battle,
and they pridefully survive a while.
Some are defeated, and they vanish from
the chronicles, the planetary scene.
Some leave great epic poems, and some have not
one opera to be remembered by.
   There's no binding equality except
what soft-eyed Shakespeare held his mirror up
to show us—our shared common creature-hood:
we thirst, we hunger, we excrete, need warmth;
we sleep, and ah! we dream. Cut us, we bleed,
and tickle our inviting ribs, we laugh.
Our bones are breakable. We breathe free air;
we work, we age, we suffer, and we die,
all of us do, we die, no one escapes—
one fate provides equality enough,
enabling us to weep for all, for everyone.

   And I am brother to the stalking wolf;
I'm sister to the fox who peeps out from
the cemetery portion of the hill.
I am the short-eared owl who perches in
the bristling needles of a tamarack
as he bears witness to the moonlit shadows
creeping through the forest on crisp snow.

Sometimes there is soft music in the air,
and I can hear your measured voice, Sweet Bard,
expressed in its component instruments:
in the wild merriment of silver flutes,
in undulating oboe warblings,
liquid clarinet remembrances,
the fading past reordered and restored,
then vanishing again in melody,
serene with momentary peacefulness.

And yet disputing forefathers still vex
my thoughts: how can we live with one another,
keeping promises, and keeping faith
in our emerging and our origins?
We lock in our key influences, our humungous treasures.
Words, and more words!
We don't know what we do not know, although
we feel wordlessly at liberty
when we accept primal dependency:
our infant cries of mortal loneliness,
that we need air, need water, sunlight, time—
strange gift of unrelenting entropy.

And you, dear wife of almost sixty years,
still fragrant with night-filling Cereus blooms,
you might have chosen someone richer, taller,
swifter, consummately smooth and suave,
someone from upscale, posh Park Avenue
and not the ethnic, gang-tormented Bronx,
a Protestant from the majority—
safe but without my repertoire
of boastfully humbling Jewish jokes.

It's sure I'm better, fellow citizen,
at being truly equal than you are.
And I declare that we with luck endure
by choosing to be who we are, resigned,
like stone George Washington upon his horse,
steadfast in the pursuit of happiness.

EVENT HORIZON

The Event Horizon—
beyond which light cannot escape
and even the reverberating past
empties out its secrecies.
Even the consciousness of consciousness is lost,
and lost the memory of memory.

Here at the edge, the final precipice,
I see my gentle friend,
his arm stretched out,
his fingertip now touching mine.
And yet his gentleness—as he repeats my name—
cannot resist the separating pull
toward nothingness
in this excruciating tenderness
of the terminal farewell.

The momentary cure for anguished thought
is deeper thought: the balm of a September afternoon,
golden chrysanthemums along an arbor entryway,
browsing deer beside a waterfall,
as if one mildly passing day
can procreate another,
and one friend's death can make
another death superfluous,
so gentleness would triumph in the end,
free from the wail of opposition
or the cry of disbelief.

Suspended in what yet remains
of my long life's elapsed eternity,
here on the precipice,
I now foresee my friend curl inward
rounding to a smooth reflecting tear,
poised and complete,
upon the cheek of wordless night.

ACKNOWLEDGMENTS

When I think on thee, dear friend,
All losses are restored and sorrows end
—SHAKESPEARE

Pat Burke
Talli Ebin
John Elder
John Glendenning
John Hunt
Gary Margolis
Paul Mariani
Dennis O'Brien
Sean O'Brien
Jay Parini
Dan Spencer
And to my sister, Marian Howard.
For James Zanze with gratitude
and abiding friendship.

CREDITS

Waking To My Name, Johns Hopkins Press, 1980.
Faces In A Single Tree, Godine, Publisher, 1984.
Clayfeld Rejoices, Clayfeld Laments, Godine, Publisher, 1987.
Before It Vanishes, Godine, Publisher, 1989.
Inheritance, Godine, Publisher, 1992.
Fathering The Map, University of Chicago Press, 1993.
Minding The Sun, University of Chicago Press, 1996.
Rounding It Out, University of Chicago Press, 1999.
Elk In Winter, University of Chcago Press, 2004.
Composing Voices, Lost Horse Press, 2005.
Still Here, Still Now, University of Chicago Press, 2008.
Laughter Before Sleep, University of Chicago Press, 2011.
To Love That Well, Lost Horse Press, 2013.
Clayfeld Holds On, University of Chicago Press, 2015.
All One Breath, Green Writers Press, 2019.

ABOUT THE AUTHOR

Robert Pack's (born 1929) long career as a teacher has included Barnard College, Middlebury College, the Middlebury College Graduate School of English, the Davidson Honors College at the University of Montana (where he received a Distinguished Teacher Award in 2008), and the Bread Loaf Writer's Conference where he was director for 22 years. This culminating collection, *Event Horizon: New and Selected Later Poems*, is his twentieth volume of poetry, which the poet Marvin Bell has described as "both heartbreaking and reassuring. One can learn from these poems how to survive."

CPSIA information can be obtained
at www.ICGtesting.com
Printed in the USA
JSHW020440281221
21589JS00001B/4